Great

MindWare®

Brainy Toys for Kids of All Ages®

Book of
Optical
Illusions

10 9 8 7 6 5 4 3 2

Published by Sterling Publishing Co., Inc.
387 Park Avenue South, New York, NY 10016
This book is comprised of material from the following Sterling titles:
BrainStrains™ BrainSnack® Puzzles © 2002 by Frank Coussement &
Peter De Schepper
BrainStrains™ Great Color Optical Illusions © 2002 by Keith Kay
Eye-Popping Optical Illusions © 2001 by Michael A. DiSpezio
Optical Illusion Magic © 1999 by Michael A. DiSpezio

© 2003 by Sterling Publishing Co., Inc.

Designed by Liz Trovato

ISBN 1-4027-1128-X

Great

Brainy Toys for Kids of All Ages®

Book of
Optical
Illusions

Michael DiSpezio,
Frank Coussement, Peter De Schepper &
Keith Kay

MindWare®
Brainy Toys for Kids of All Ages®

CONTENTS

INTRODUCTION

No matter what age you are—optical illusions are cool. People are always drawn to their magic and eye-popping wow.

Optical illusions of one kind or another have been part of the human experience throughout all of time. Whether you are gazing at the moon and a face appears or trekking through the desert and encounter a mirage, these experiences are at once familiar and fascinating. These tricks of the mind and eye certainly raised questions and got the imagination going. Ultimately, such elements were used to develop techniques in art, lighting, and architecture. Think of the shadows and play with colors that a painter employs to display perspective of an object. Look at the architecture of great

buildings and how illusions are used to enhance their appearance.

Some of the optical illusions in this collection will be more straightforward than others. Some will ask questions about a picture just to encourage you to view it differently. Others will ask compelling questions pertaining to the images and will give answers. Some will not.

Optical Illusion fanatics not only enjoy the visual challenge of the puzzles, but also benefit by learning how to problem solve and think in a whole new light.

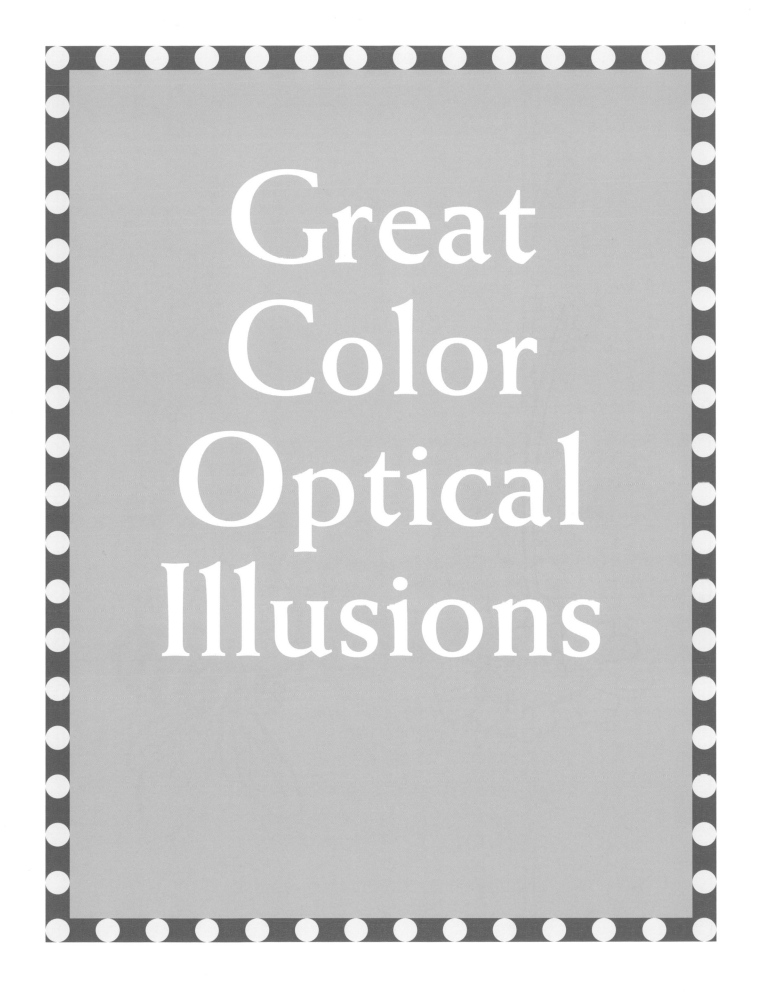

Great
Color
Optical
Illusions

What do you see in this strange picture?

Is the zebra black with white stripes or
is it white with black stripes?

Slowly rotate this page in a circular motion. What happens to the clown's drum? What's unusual about the word "rotator"?

The name of this old-time print is
"Time Passes." Why do you think it
was given this title?

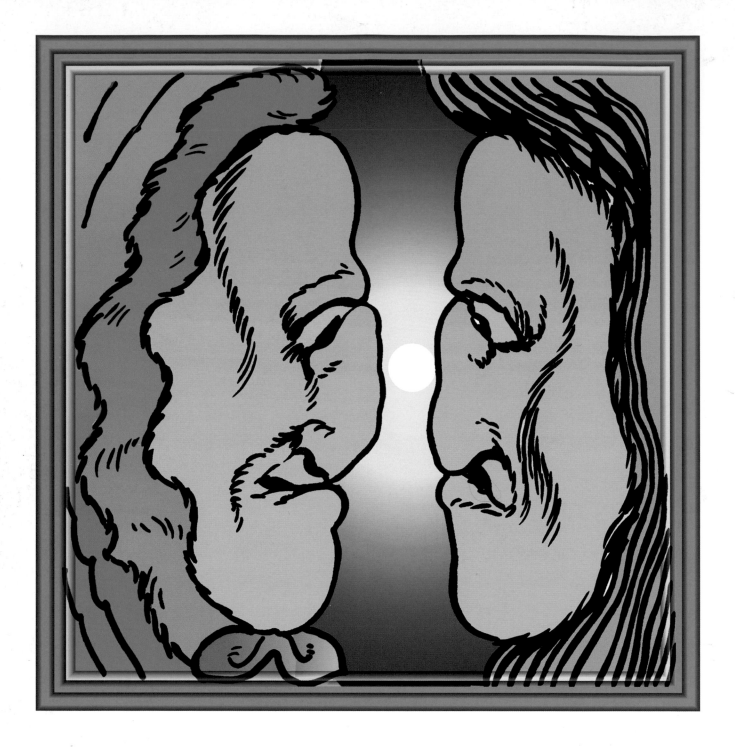

Can you figure out why this picture is
titled "Before and After Marriage"?

This picture shows a young girl and her grandmother.
Can you find both of them?

How can you get the bee to move closer to the flower?

Place a pencil along the line of the two arrows.
What happens to the color of the circle?

What playing card is represented in this illustration?

Stare at the red dot for about 30 seconds. Try not to blink. Then look at a blank wall or a sheet of whitepaper. You will see a famous lady. Who is she?

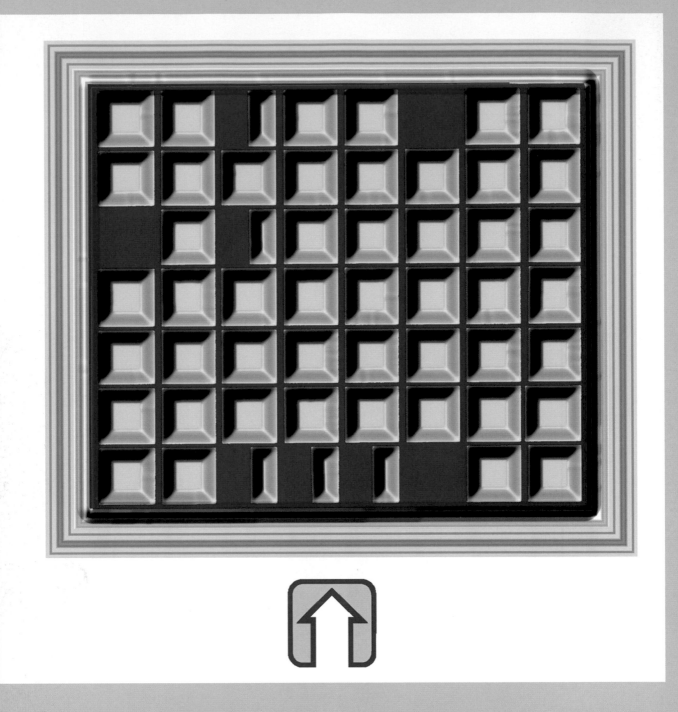

Can you discover the secret word that has been concealed in this design?

MADAM I'M ADAM

Do you notice anything unusual about this eaten apple?
The clue is in the phrase.
What's unusual about the phrase?

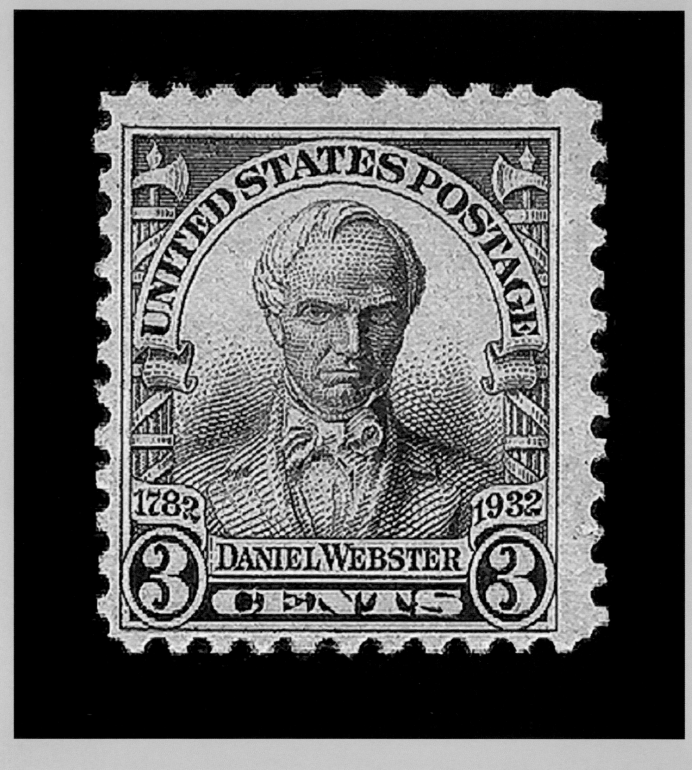

This is a real postage stamp of Daniel Webster. If you turn it upside down and look very carefully, you will see someone else. Who do you see?

Can you figure out what these shapes represent?

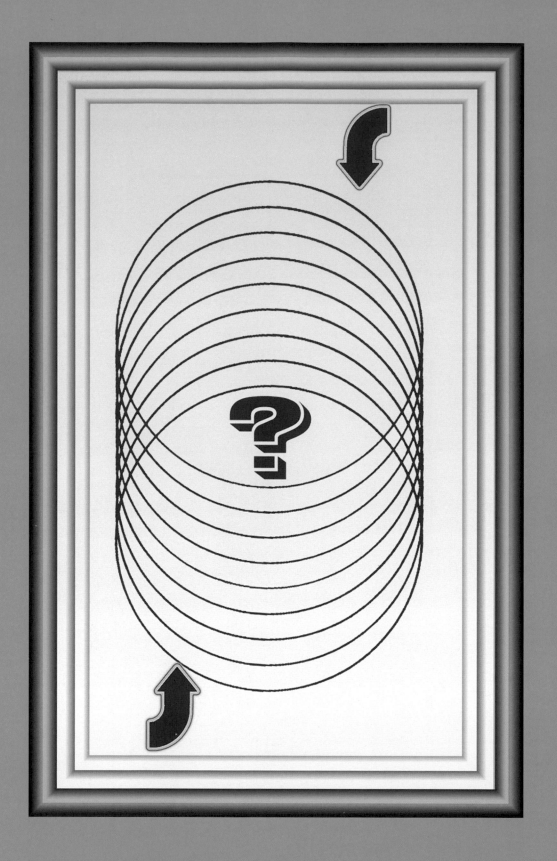

You can look through this coil from either end.
Keep staring at it and what happens?

Otto is holding a cake. One slice is missing. Can you find it?
There is also something odd about the name "Otto." What is it?

Are these two painted stripes exactly the same size,
or is one bigger than the other?

IT'S MAGIC !

96	11	89	68
88	69	91	16
61	86	18	99
19	98	66	81

What's so special about this set of numbers?

What do you see in this picture?

What do you see in this picture:
Blue arrows or yellow arrows?

What is this a picture of?

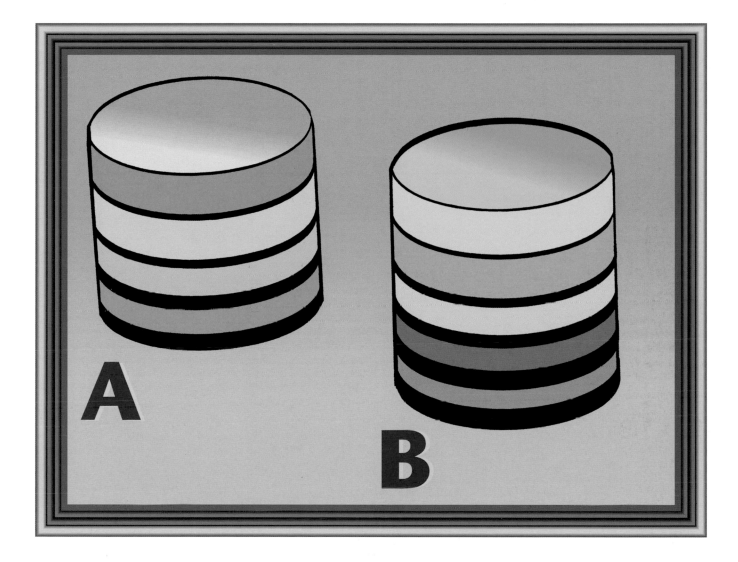

Which pile of disks has the same height and width?

The soldier is pointing his finger straight at you.
Move your head from left to right. What appears to happen?

This soldier is looking for his horse.
Do you have any idea where it is?

What happens when you rotate this
page in a circular motion?

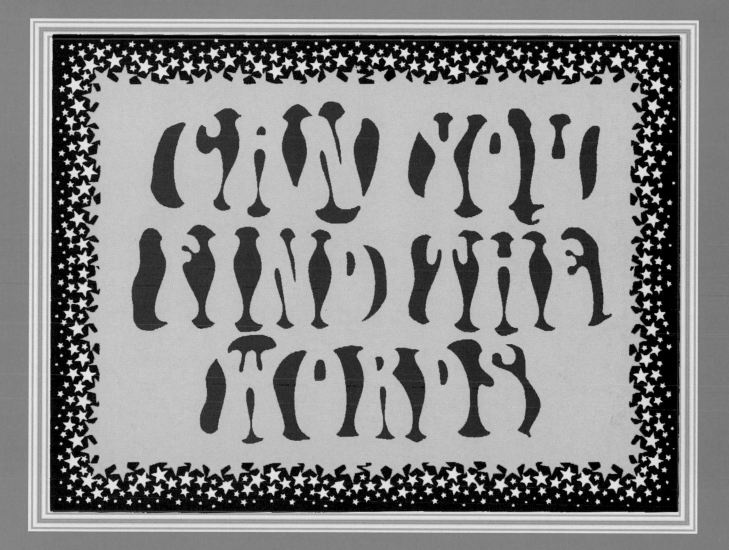

Can you find the hidden message?
What does it say?

Can you find this baby's mother?

This old sketch is called "Under the Mistletoe."
What's odd about this drawing?

The sailor is looking through his telescope to find his girlfriend.
Can you find her?

BACCHUS

This is a picture of the Roman god Bacchus. If you look very carefully you will also see a picture of Romeo and Juliet. Can you find them?

This mathematical problem is wrong. How can you correct it?

Sherlock Holmes is reading a headline. What does it say?
Are you sure?

This is a poster of vaudeville performer, T. Elder Hearn. He was a
quick-change artist. What do you see in this publicity print?

The brown shapes may seem unrelated, but they form a figure.
It is an example of a "closure." Can you see what the figure is?

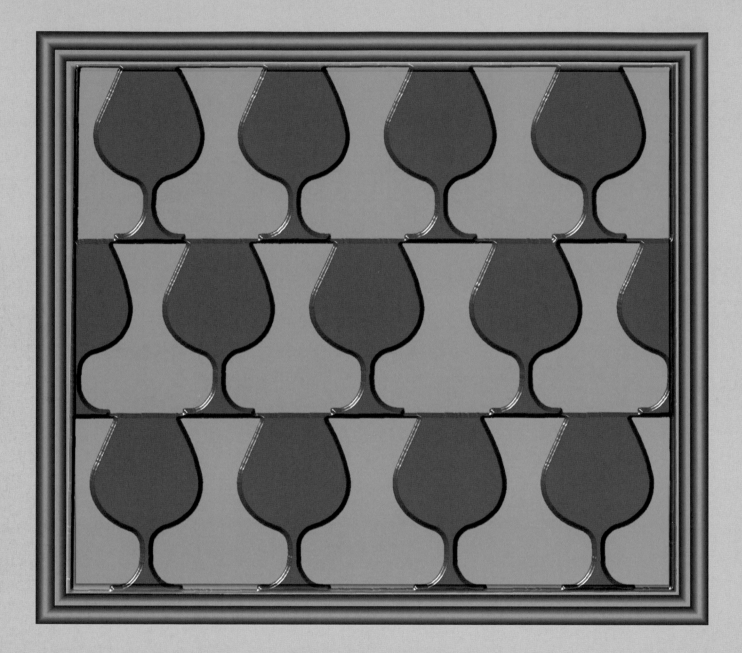

What do you see, purple glasses or green vases?

Does this sign say "knowledge" or does it say "ignorance"?

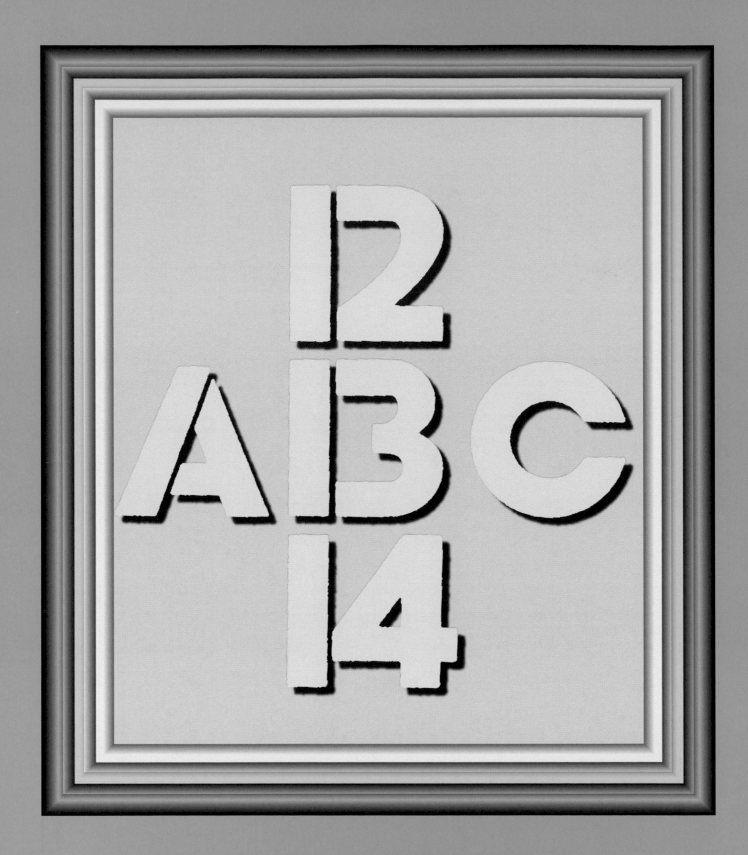

What do you see in the middle of the frame?
Is it the letter B or the number 13?

The shop was selling poor-quality dice at 50¢ each.
This was not the correct price. Can you figure out what was the real price?

How can you get the boy to take a spoonful of his medicine?

Read the words in the hat very slowly. What do they say?

At first glance, we see a pig. But where is the farmer?

Observe this cow very carefully.
Do you notice anything unusual about it?

Using only your eyes, count the number of F's in the above sentence. How many are there?

Can you spot the farmer in this landscape?

Can you see where Napoleon is hiding?

Napoleon's supporters used to wear violets as a sign of their allegiance.
This print hides the faces of Napoleon, Maria Louisa, and the
young king of Rome. Can you find them?

This attractive landscape print holds a secret.
Can you find the landlord?

This is the island of St. Helena. Where is Napoleon?

Can you discover why this old British colonial patriotic design is called
"The Glory of a Lion Is His Mane"?

What is unusual about this sentence?

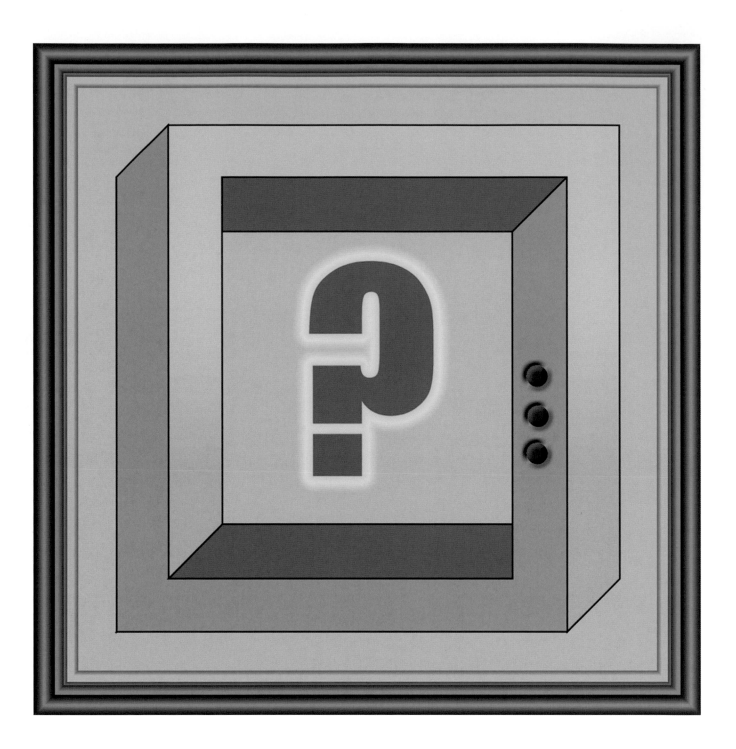

Are the three dots on the inside or the outside of this frame?

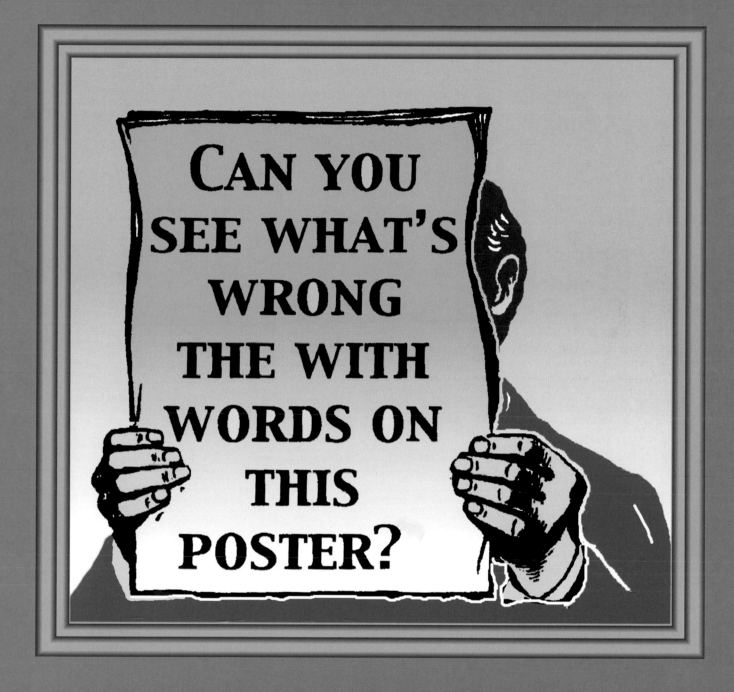

Can you see what's wrong with this poster?

What is strange about these donkeys?

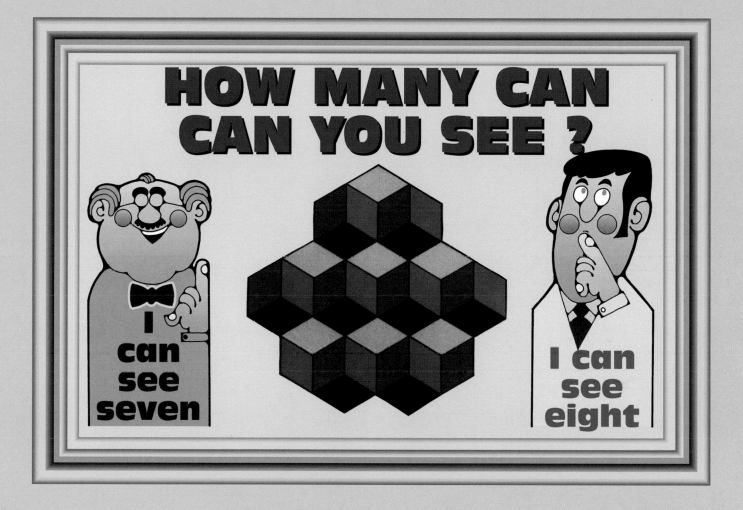

How many cubes can you see, seven or eight?

What's wrong with this picture?

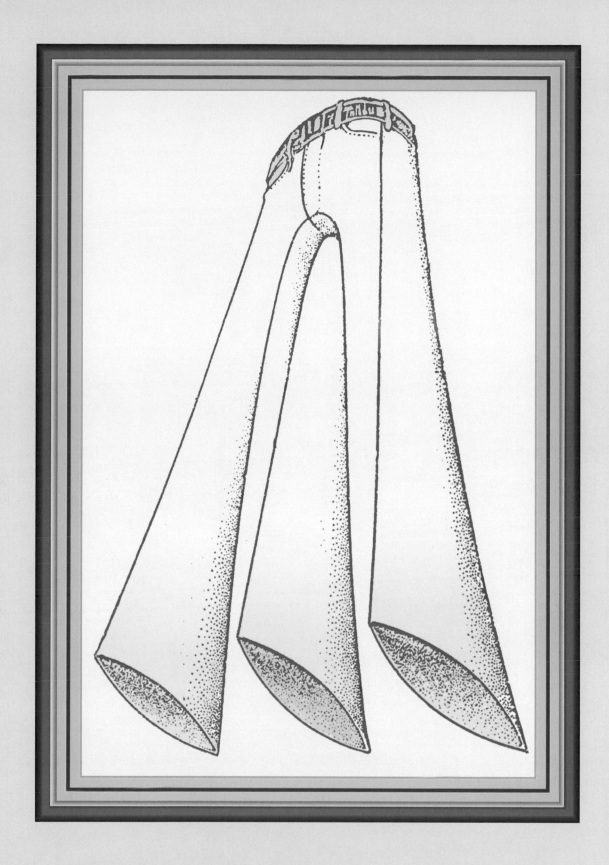

Can you see what's wrong with this pair of bell-bottoms?

Turn the page upside down and you will see that the year 1961 still says 1961.
When was the last "upside down" year and when will the next one occur?

The farmer's son was adding up the large number of eggs laid over a 3-week period. Do you see anything unusual about the answer?

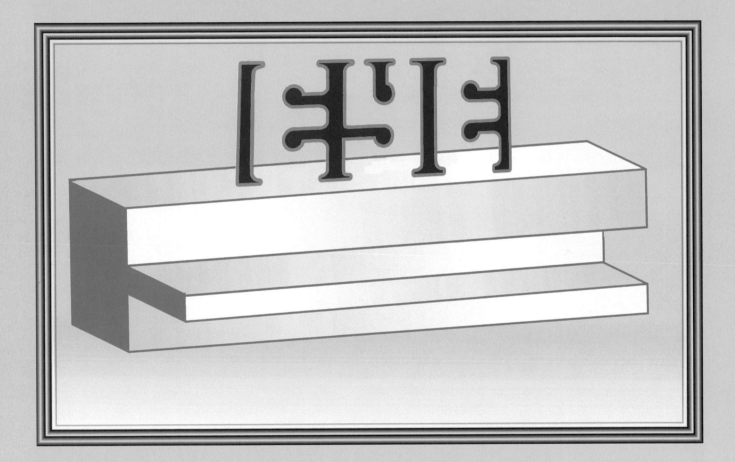

Can you figure out the meaning of the shapes on the top shelf?
And what's unusual about the structure?

A farmer put up this sign. Can you understand what he was trying to say?

Stare at the yellow dot for about 30 seconds. Try not to blink.
Now stare at a piece of white paper. What do you see?

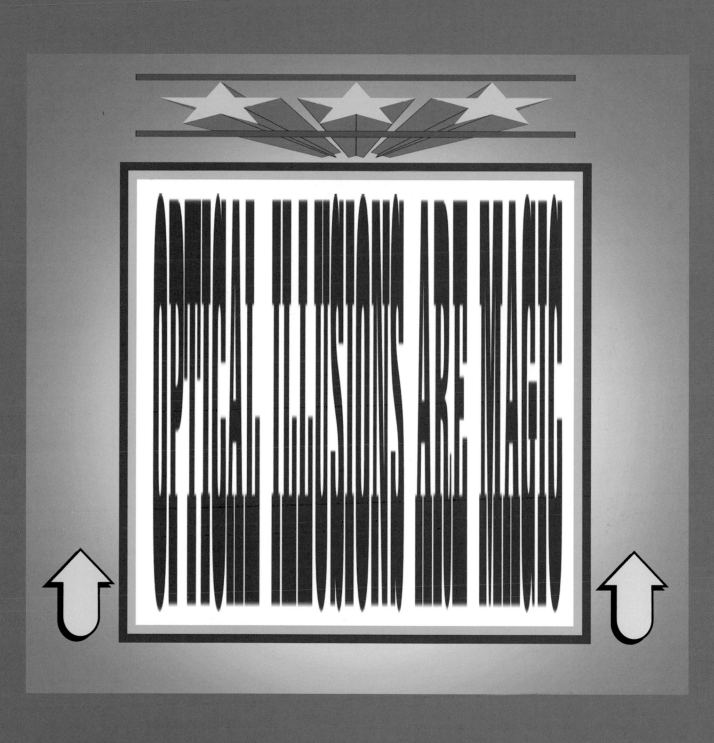

Can you read this secret message? Tilt the page to eye level and look in the direction of the arrows with one eye closed.

What bird do you see here, a hawk or a goose?

CLOWNING AROUND

Clowns work in the circus. Here's the clown. Where's the circus?

Can you figure out what this Victorian puzzle shows? Is it an animal, vegetable, or mineral? Try looking at it from different angles.

Look carefully at this dog. Can you find its master?

Do you notice anything unusual about this flight of steps?

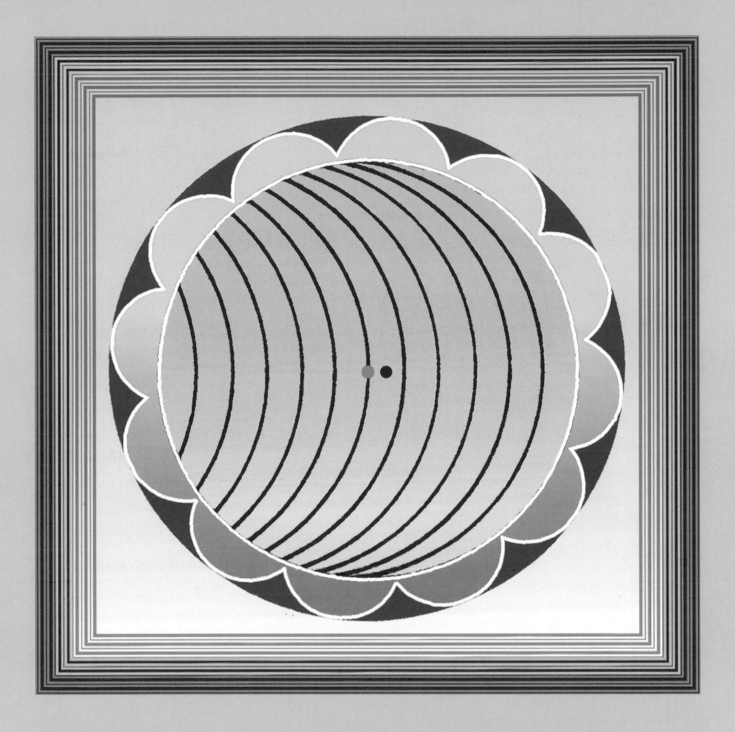

Which of these two dots is in the true center?

Is the star closer to the top or the base of the mountain?

What do you see in this picture?

Will the girl ever get to the bottom step on this flight of stairs?

Magician Horace Goldin used this flyer to advertise his theater shows. Who looks taller, Goldin as a man or as a boy?

Without turning the page upside down, describe this man.
Is he happy or sad? Now check to find out.

Only one of these sets of letters says something when viewed in a mirror.
Can you figure out which one it is before using the mirror?

The hooded monk has a bizarre secret. What is it?

How do you turn a duck into a rabbit?

This picture is based on what were known in Victorian times as "Fantasy Faces." What do you see?

Is there life after death?

ADD OR SUBTRACT?

Have you ever mixed colors of paint? If so, you know that by mixing the right colors you can produce a limitless assortment of shades. As different pigments are added to the mixture, they absorb certain colors, which takes away from the total light reflected off the paint. This "taking away" process is called subtractive mixing of colors.

Mixing colored lights is a completely different story. When colored lights are shown on the same spot, no colors are taken away. In fact, as different colors of light are added, the amount of reflected light increases. This process is known as additive mixing of colors.

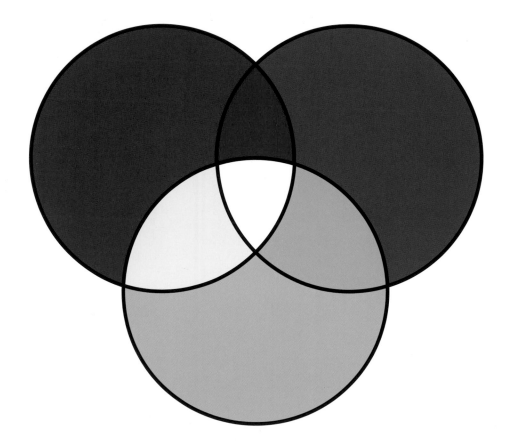

Here's what happens when red, green, and blue lights are mixed together. The additive properties combine to form more colors.

Eye Popping Optical Illusions

EQUAL STACK

Examine the three stacks below. One stack has a height (measured from upper edge A to lower edge B) equal to its width. Which one is it?

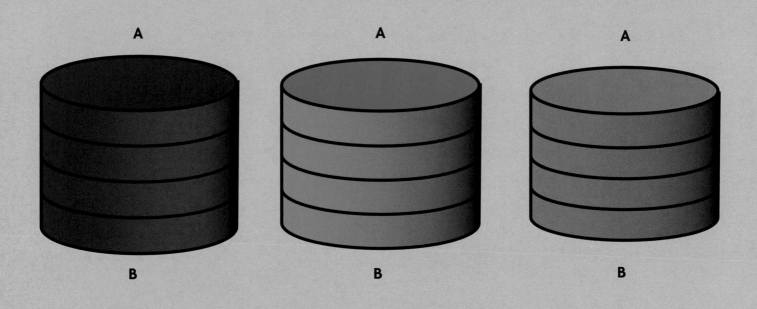

The first stack has the equal dimensions. It probably doesn't appear that way because several optical tricks are at work. The first twist is that we ordinarily tend to stretch objects to make them appear somewhat taller than what they actually are. The second twist has to do with the 3-D appearance of the stacks. This extra processing further confuses your perception. The third has to do with the extra length we tack onto the stacks because of the printed letters.

TWISTED OUTLOOK

You don't need curved lines to twist an appearance. Notice how this pattern of triangles tricks your brain into seeing slightly slanted walls.

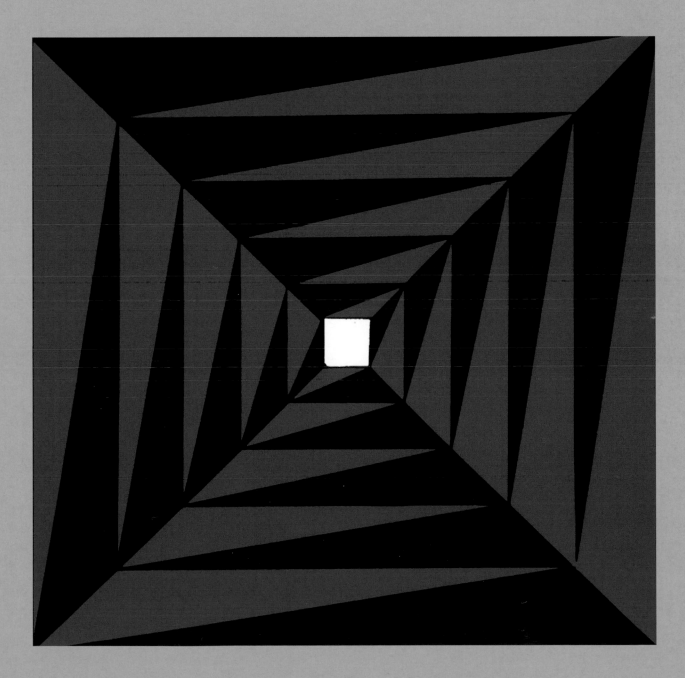

FILL 'ER UP

Which square appears tallest?

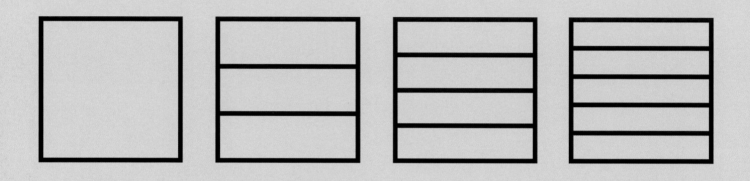

The square with the most lines probably appears tallest. Although all four squares are the same size, the "fill" tricks your brain into overestimating the dimensions.

POP GOES THE FIGURE

What's in this image?
1. Four white hour glasses
2. Small black four-blade pinwheel
3. Larger white four-blade pinwheel

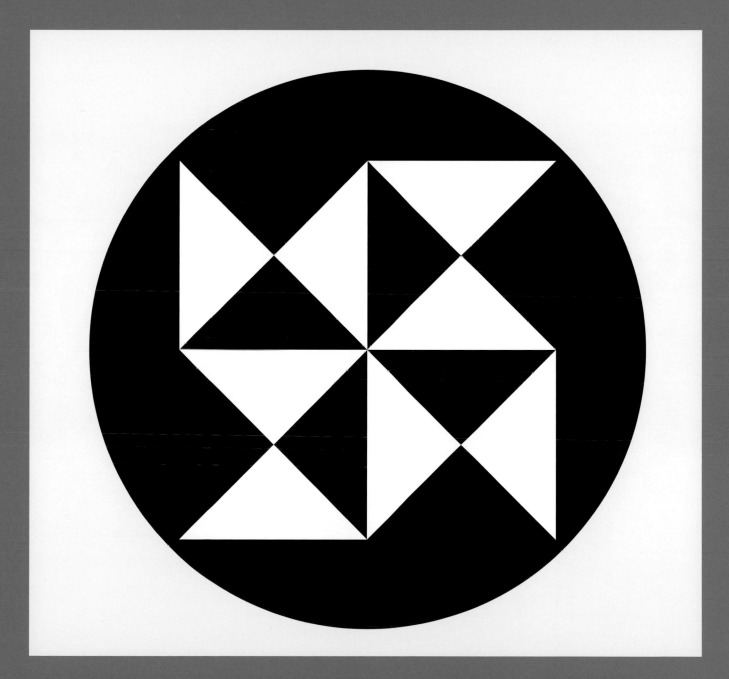

Any and all of the shapes mentioned can be found in this image. It depends upon what parts of the background you "pop" into the foreground.

CLUTTER

Have you ever searched a messy room looking for a missing toy? Finally, just as you are about to give up, the toy appears right in plain sight. Although it was there all this time, the toy was hidden by clutter. Your eyes detect its shape, but your brain doesn't assemble a clear view of the scene.

Now here's another hidden view that's in plain sight. Can you identify the subject of this splattered picture?

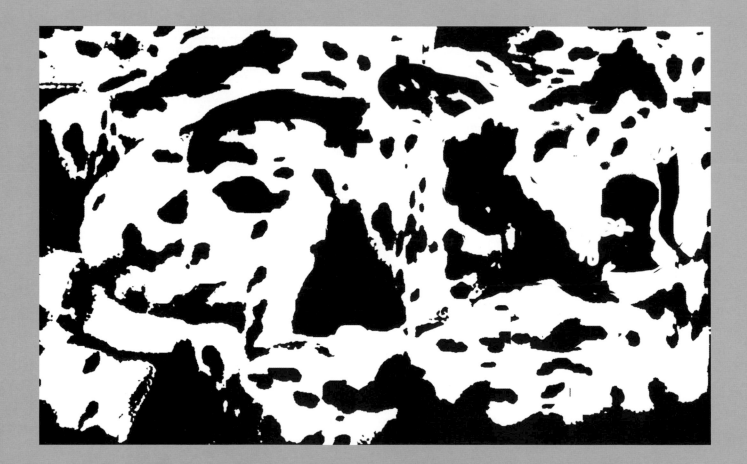

It's a Dalmatian curled up on the ground. Its nose is off to the right. Its curled tail is on the left.

CATCHING Z's

This pattern is formed by rows of Z's that are tilted in three different directions. Can you uncover all three tilts? Can you see all three tilts at once or must you "switch" from one slope to another?

Most people will see only one, or perhaps two, of the slopes very quickly, but they will have a difficult time seeing the third slope. Once they do, people have to switch "attention gears" in order to see each of the three slopes. Most people will not see all three at the same time.

STANDING OUT

Take a look at this pattern of three blocks. What do you see?

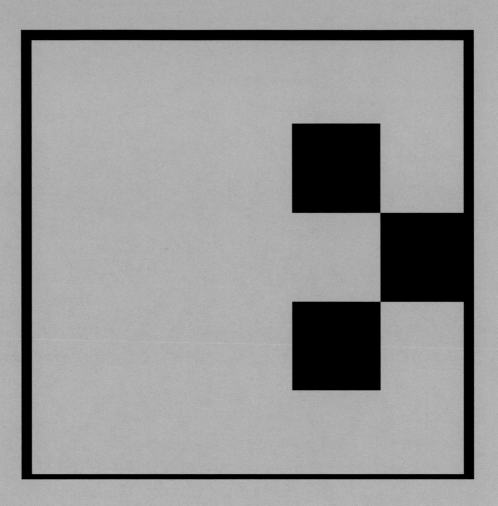

Do you see the letter E? Although it might be difficult to see the E at first, you'll have no problem in finding it now that you know what to expect. This pattern has been recorded into your visual experience and processing record book.

HOLY SPOKES!

Hold this page upright and spin it in small, tight circles. Don't spin it too fast. Keep looking at the center of this pattern. Do you see the illusionary spiral spokes that appear to race around the circles? How does the direction of the spoke movement compare with the direction of the book spin?

No one knows for certain why we see these spokes, but some psychologists believe it has to do with confused communication between the cells in our eyes.

HIGHS AND LOWS OF LIGHT

Does this pattern of rings appear to open towards the upper left or lower right? Most people will first see the rings as pointing towards the upper left. But keep looking at the center. The appearance will soon flip towards the lower right.

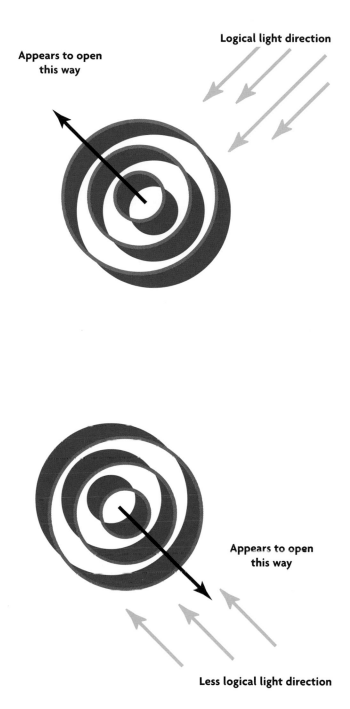

Logical light direction

Appears to open this way

Appears to open this way

Less logical light direction

The image is drawn so that it can be viewed either way. However, lighting cues suggest that the rings pointing towards the upper left are more logical than the rings pointing to the lower right.

Most of the time light comes to us from above through such sources as the sun, ceiling fixtures, and streetlights. Because we are used to that, we interpret scenes using this lighting angle.

If we imagine that a light is placed above our 3-D ring pattern, it must be located to the upper right. Therefore, the rings appear to open to the upper left. Since this is a logical position for a light, we have a tendency to interpret the image in this orientation.

A less logical position for a light source is to have it come up from the lower right. Only after we look at this image for several seconds will this alternate orientation emerge.

BOXED IN BY THE LIGHT

Describe this shape.

This is another image that can present two logical appearances. What it looks like depends on the direction you assign to the light source. If the light comes from above, the image looks like a simple cube that has its top corner missing. If, however, you assume that the light comes from below, it appears to be a small box that is positioned in the corner of a ceiling.

VIBRATING VISUALS

Back in the 1960s, Op Art was very popular. This illustration style used highly contrasting shapes and patterns to produce a sensation of movement called visual vibration. Look into this figure and you'll see that many of the edges appear to have an "electric" or glowing quality.

RISE AND SINK

The red or blue box can seem to be on top of the stack.
Can you switch their positions in your mind?

STRIPE ONE

Take a look at the blue stripes in each of the two circles. Are they the same shade of blue or is one darker than the other?

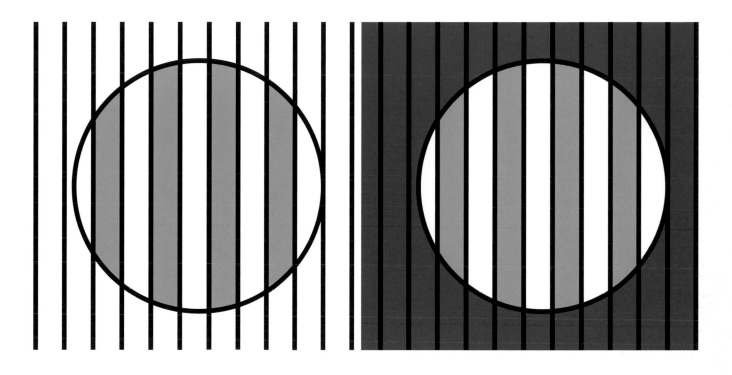

Although they don't appear it, the stripes in each of the circles are the exact same shade. It's the blue background behind the second circle that sends your brain on to a faulty shortcut. Against this darker surrounding, the inner stripes of the second circle look brighter and so your brain retains this concept of "bright" when it compares the shades of the stripes.

PURPLE SQUARES

These two purple squares are:
a. The exact same size (only one is rotated on its side)
b. The same shade of purple
c. Slightly different sizes
d. Slightly different shades of purple
e. Both a and b
f. Both c and d

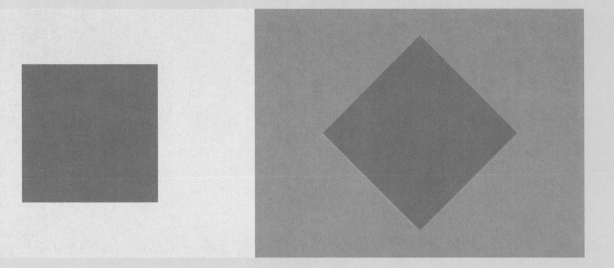

Believe it or not, the correct answer is e—both purple squares are the exact same shade and size. The different shades of gray create an unfair comparison background. Your brain incorrectly processes the purple surrounded by the darker background as a light shade. In addition, the rotated appearance of a square makes it appear larger.

RING

Take a close look at this ring. Is the top half the same thickness as the bottom half? Or is the bottom half slightly thicker? Is the shade the same around the entire ring or is half of it printed in a slightly different shade?

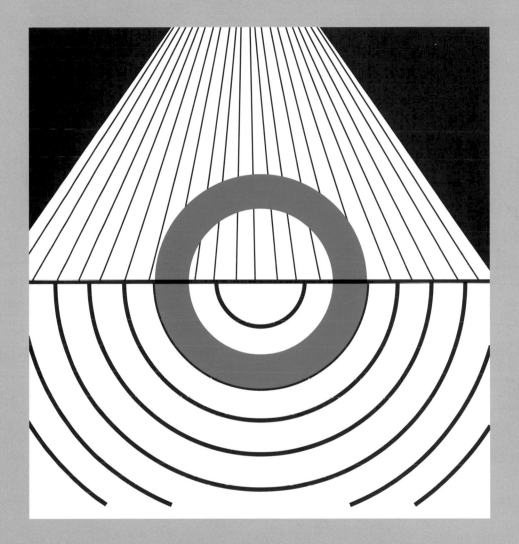

The top and bottom halves of the ring are the same thickness. Use a ruler and you'll discover that their width is the same. In addition, the ring is printed in the same shade throughout its length.

Two illusions are at work here. The distortions in size and shading are produced by the background patterns. These patterns lead your visual processing astray and suggest a false sense of 3-D. They also offer an inconsistent background for comparison.

DOT DITTO DEMYSTIFIED

Relax and overlap these rows of images. If you can't free view this effect, use paper tubes to help fuse the image pairs. What do you see?

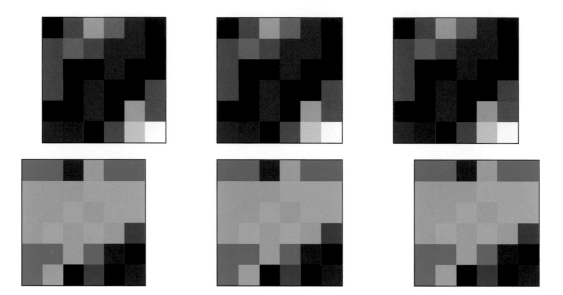

The squares overlap and produce the illusion of 3-D. Keep examining the scene. To most people, the upper row of three squares appears to float somewhat higher than the lower row. This difference in percieved height is caused by the difference in separation distance.

   The squares of the upper row are closer together. The squares in the lower row are wider apart. When the squares in both rows are overlapped, this difference between the images creates the illusion of different planes.

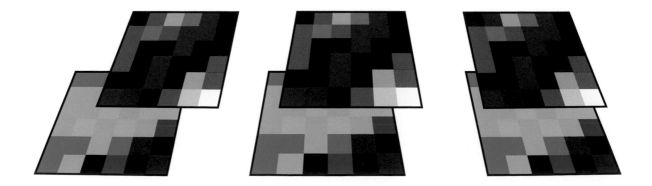

STEREOGRAM

Take a look at the "random" dot stereoimage below. Can you see a pattern within the jumble of dots?

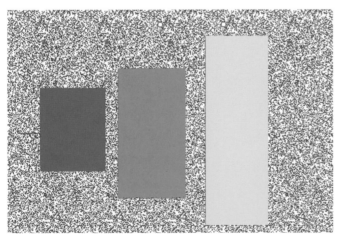

The pattern that is embedded into the dot placement is a very simple arrangement of rectangles. This basic view is easier to see than the more complex stereodot images. Here's what the pop-up pattern looks like.

WHAT WE SEE

Looking at the target, each eye captures a slightly different view of it as shown at the right.

Apply your free viewing technique on these two images. Relax. As these images fuse together, your brain goes at it again and creates the illusion of depth. If needed, use your viewing tubes to help achieve this effect.

Left-eye view

Right-eye view

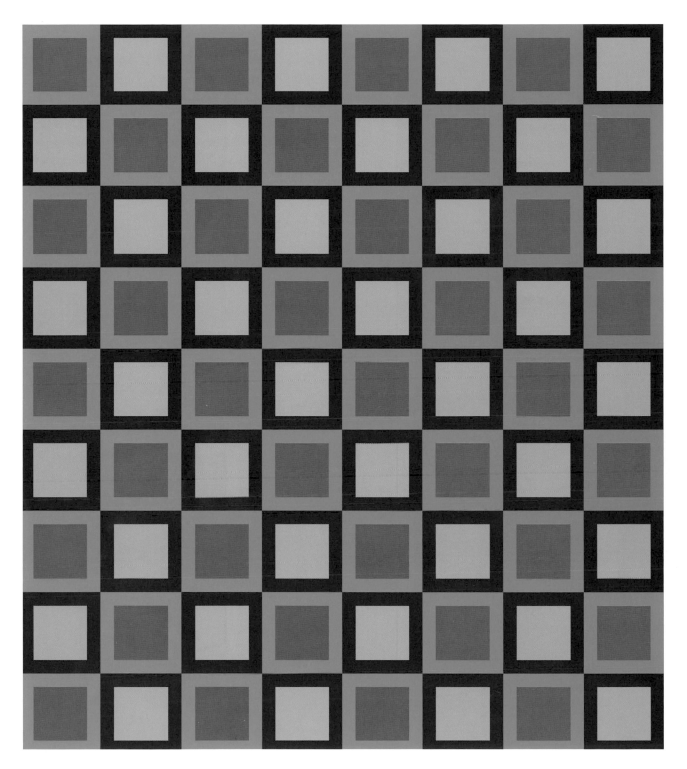

Are these stacks of square blocks perfectly vertical?

At close range, you can see that this pattern is made up of circles. But what happens to these circles when you hold the page at a distance?

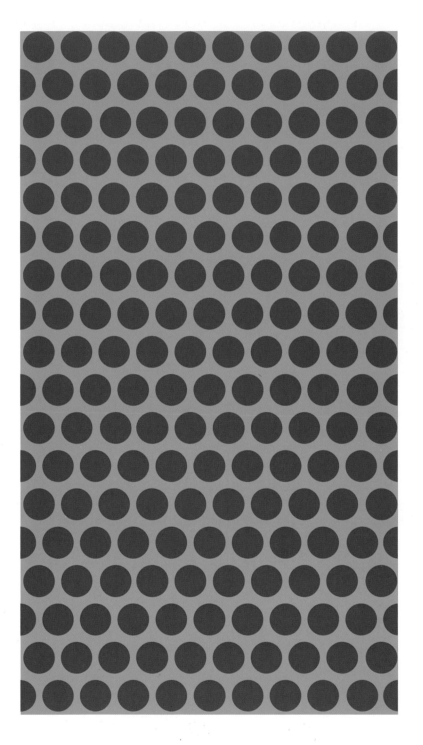

Two changes in appearance occur. First, you organize this featureless pattern into familiar shapes, such as triangles, hexagons, rows, columns, and slanted lines. Second, the circles change their shape into six-sided figures called hexagons.

FAST FLOWER FIND

How fast can you uncover the flower that is missing a single petal?

Even though there were three hundred flowers, you spotted the odd image within seconds! This ability to uncover things that stick out is wired into your visual processing ability.

DOT DILEMMA

Take a look at the patterns shown on these two pages. You probably have very little difficulty in identifying the colors printed here. Now prop up this book so this spread remains open. Walk to the far side of the room. Don't look at the book while you're moving. At the opposite end of the room, look at these patterns again. What do you see?

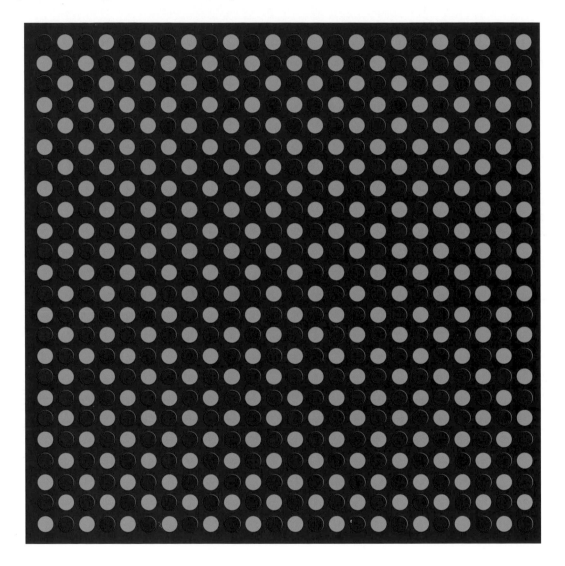

What color do you think this pattern of blue and yellow dots will appear when viewed from across the room?

The image is now yellow! At a distance, the red and green dots are no longer distinct. Their light blends together. The red cones and green cones react to the light. Because they can't focus on the individual dots, they see the entire image as a blur and your brain processes the mixture of color as yellow.

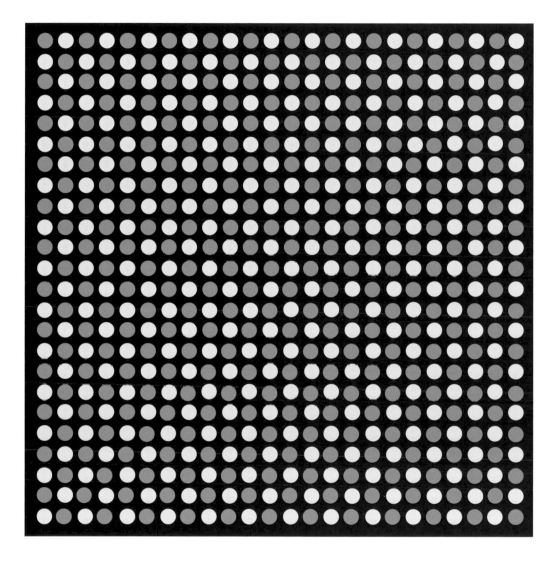

The image is now green.

Take a look at this blob of red. Gently move the page back and forth in a swirling motion. Does the blob remain the same or does it look wobbly?

PERFECTLY PROBLEMATIC PILLARS

These columns are perfectly straight, vertical, and parallel to each other. The slanted lines drawn in the columns create a false sense of 3-D. Your misguided visual processing goes to work and "repaints" the scene as a set of bent columns.

Optical
Illusion
Magic

TRICKY TRACKS

Take a look at the two dinosaurs. A good look! The dinosaur at the top of the tracks appears to be slightly larger than the animal at the bottom of the picture. Right?

See explanation of Tricky Tracks on page 242

The railroad track illusion also works with a photograph. Both horizontal bars are the exact same size and length! Those same misleading clues (also called cues) are at it again.

COMPARISON CONCEPTS

Which middle square is larger?

 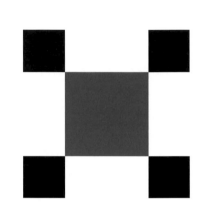

The square surrounded by the larger blocks doesn't look as big as the same sized square surrounded by smaller blocks.

See explanation of Comparison Concepts on page 242

Which center circle looks bigger?

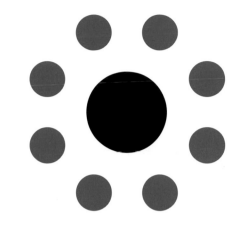

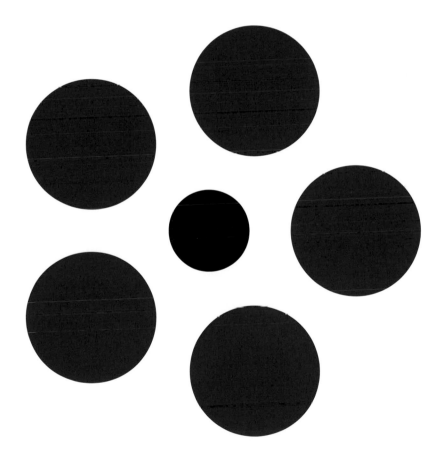

Both circles are the same size, although the one surrounded by blue dots appears bigger.

See explanation of Comparison Concepts on page 242

LEANING LAYERS

Does the pattern look warped?

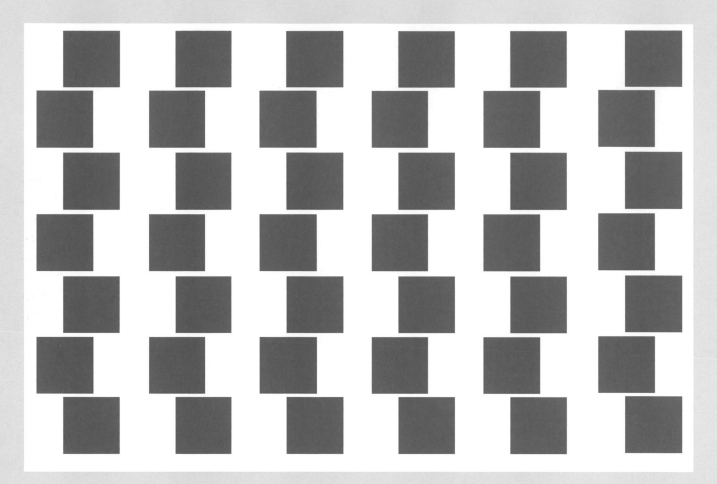

You bet it does! It's an illusion that is suggested by the offset of the blocks. The slight shift tricks your brain into "seeing" slanted layers. But do any of these slants exist? Only in your mind. Place the straight edge of a ruler beneath each line and you'll observe the perfectly straight and flat arrangement.

Here's another example:

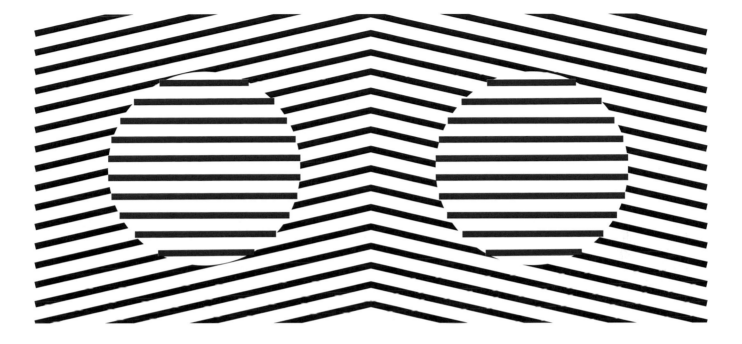

The lines in the circles are perfectly horizontal. It's the background pattern that suggests their tilt. Always open to suggestion, your brain makes a "wrong turn" and sees something different from what it actually is!

COMPARED TO WHAT?

Our sense of shade and color depends upon how an object appears against a background. Examine the two inner squares. Although they don't look it, both squares are the exact same shade of gray.

The square on the left is placed over a light background and appears dark. The square on the right is placed over a dark background. In contrast, it appears light.

SHADY COMPARISON

Look at the purple bar that stretches across the two-colored boxes. It contains a uniform shade of purple. Now, place your finger across the bar so that the whole illustration is separated into a right and left half. Does the purple appear the same on both sides of your finger?

The purple that is surrounded by the blue appears slightly brighter than the purple that remains against the pink background. This illusion is based upon a comparison of an object to its background. In this case, your brain was tricked into mistakenly "tweaking" the bar colors.

AFTER IMAGES

Stare at the center of this sign for 15 seconds. Switch your focus to the center of the blank outline below it. Does anything appear?

Stare at the center of this oddly-colored flag for 15 seconds. Switch your focus to a white wall or ceiling. Does anything more American materialize?

See explanation of After Images on page 242.

ILLUSIONARY FIGURES

Look into this pattern of spheres. Can you find the imaginary cube?

How about a four-sided pyramid?

FLIP-FLOPPING

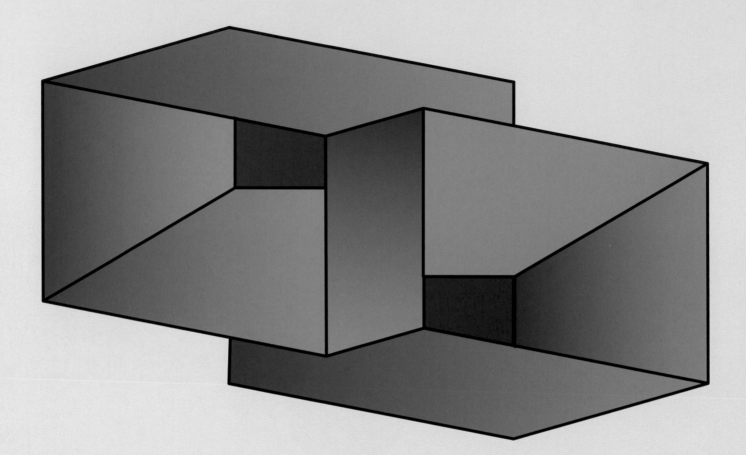

Try building these crazy crates and you'll find yourself boxed in by the laws of physics. You'll also experience how impossible figures can shift quickly between their unstable forms.

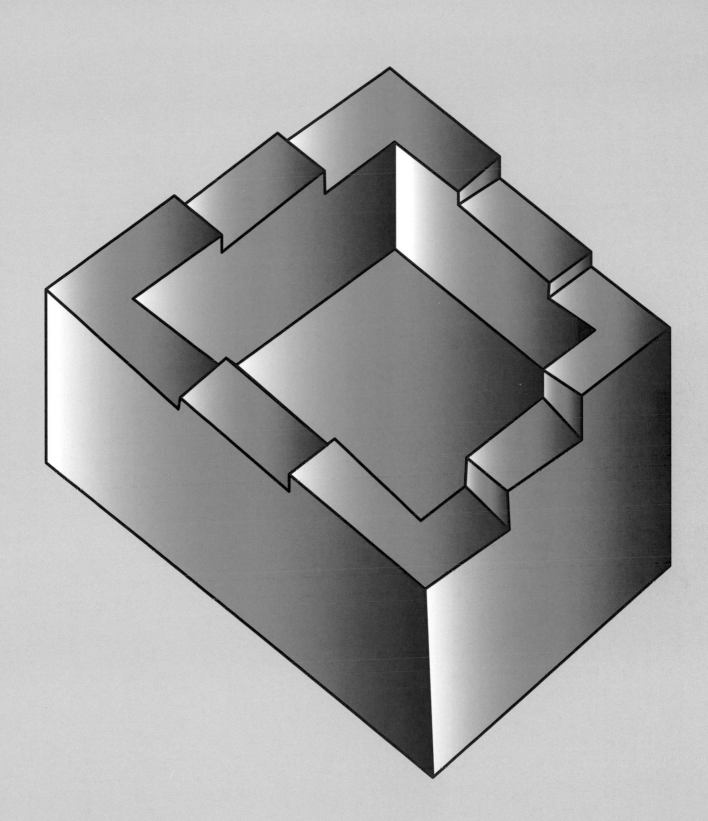

Here's a basic impossible staircase. What happens when you go up or down these stairs?

IMPOSSIBLE POSSIBILITIES

Here's a drawing of an impossible triangle. As you can see, the twists of its frame can only exist on paper. Obviously, there is no way that a triangle like this can exist as an real object—or can it?

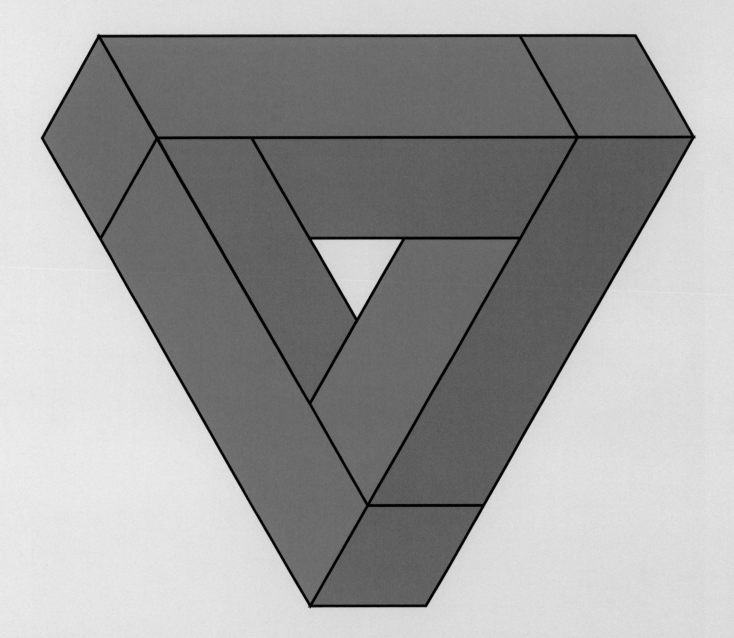

Hang on to your brains. Here's an actual and unretouched photograph of an impossible triangle! What? How can this wooden frame have impossible twists? What's going on here?

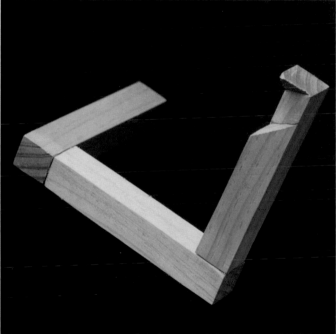

This is a real visual trick. What appears to be a closed triangle isn't. The wooden frame is bent and open. From the camera's view, however, the open ends overlap, making it appear to be a closed triangle. If we change our view, we can see what this tricky frame really looks like.

Suppose you were driving down the road and stopped at an intersection. You look up and see this sign? What does it mean?

Most people interpret this sign as four yellow arrows. The arrows appear to indicate four directions. But can you see anything else?

A few people won't see the arrows first. Instead, they see a black "H" printed over a yellow diamond. Can you make this image flip flop between these two views?

PUZZLING PATTERN

Stare at the center of this pattern as you count to five S-L-O-W-L-Y. What happens? Flip-flopping madness! Does the pattern remain stable or does it appear to shift?

NEW OUTLOOK

Can you make the 3D shape above look jump between the three forms shown below? Can you uncover other ways to "see" this figure with depth?

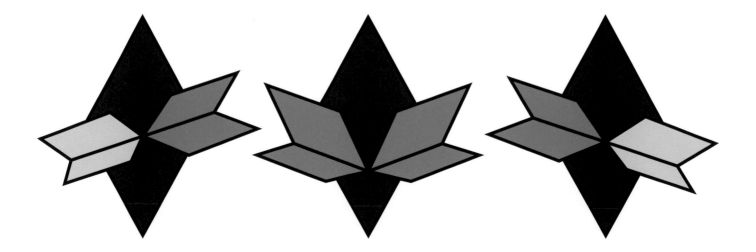

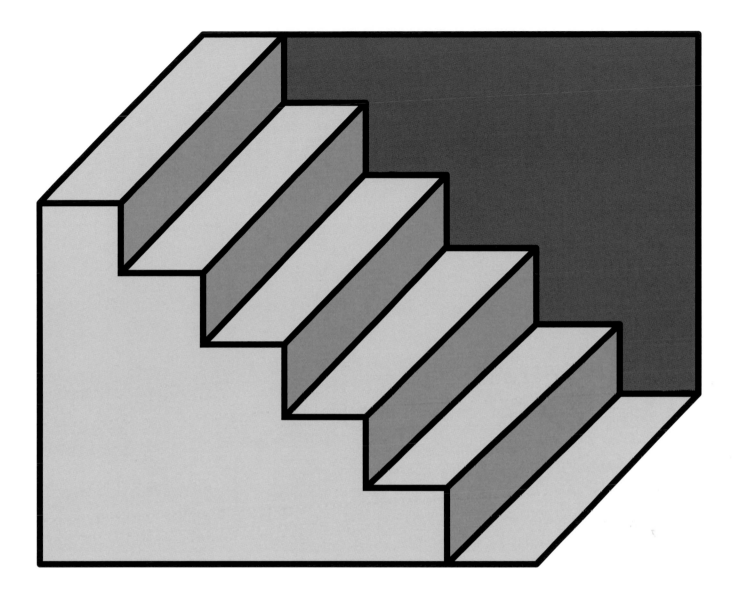

The staircase above presents little room for doubt. The four steps rise from left to right. The near side of the staircase is brown. The far wall is purple. However, it can have another appearance. Can you see this image as an overhang?

See hint for New Outlook on page 242.

THICK AS A BRICK

Most likely you saw this as a pattern of bricks lined up from the top left corner to the bottom right corner. The bright surfaces are the brick tops. But would you believe that the surfaces can also be seen as brick bottoms? It's not easy to do. To help change your outlook on this image, rotate the page upside down. The bricks pattern should "flip." Try to maintain this pattern as you rotate the page back around. It's difficult, but it can be done.

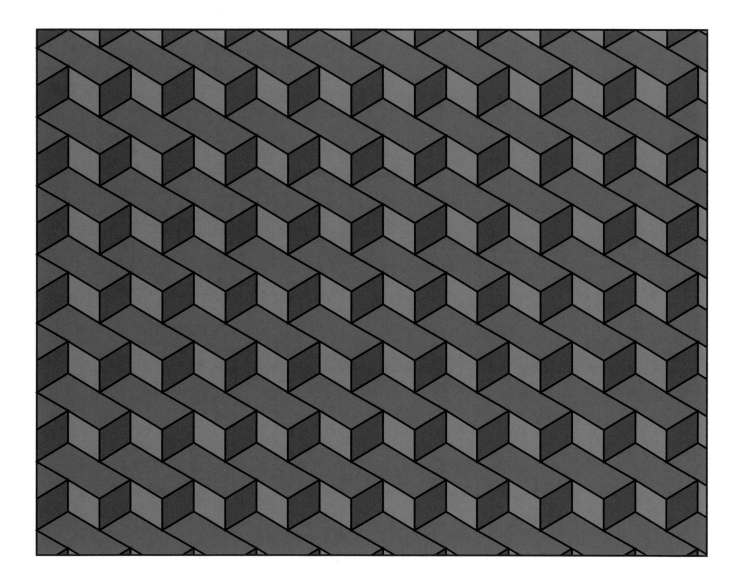

HEX MAKES THE SPOT

Stare at the center of the hexagon pattern. What happens?

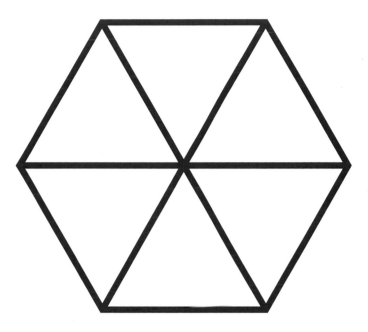

Within a few moments, your brain probably got tired of seeing a flat target. To "liven" things up, it built something with a little more depth: a cube. The near side of this object can face right or left. Can you isolate both views of the cube? How quickly can you flip the hexagon image between the two cube views?

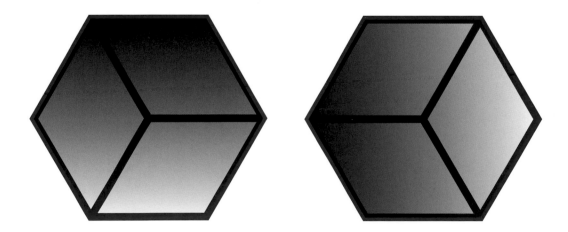

MORE FLIP-FLOPPING

A rabbit or a duck?

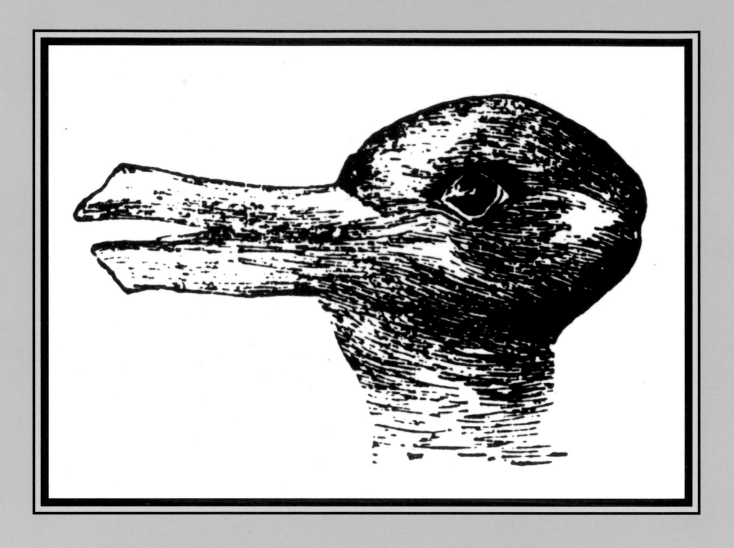

This illusion was created around the turn of the century. Its appearance flip-flops between two popular animals.

Does your previous experience affect what you see? You bet it does! If people are shown pictures of rabbits before seeing this illusion, they are more likely to see a rabbit. If, however, they are shown pictures of ducks, they are more likely to see a duck.

ABOUT FACE

Here's another flip-flopping mind boggler that appeared around the turn of the century. Can you see the profile of the Native American chief? Keep looking at this face and it will soon transform into an Inuit turned in the direction of his igloo. Can you "see" both images at the same time?

KING OF ILLUSIONS

Stare at the dot in the center of this picture for 20 seconds. Quickly switch your focus to the star in the center of the newspaper cover to the right. Who appears?

The Daily Tabloid

THE KING SEEN EVERYWHERE!

★

See explanation of After Images on page 242

Here's another illusion that you've probably seen before. It's an ambiguous figure that flip flops between two profiles and a vase.

THE CIRCLE GAME

Look at the circle below. Which color dot is placed at the center of the circle?

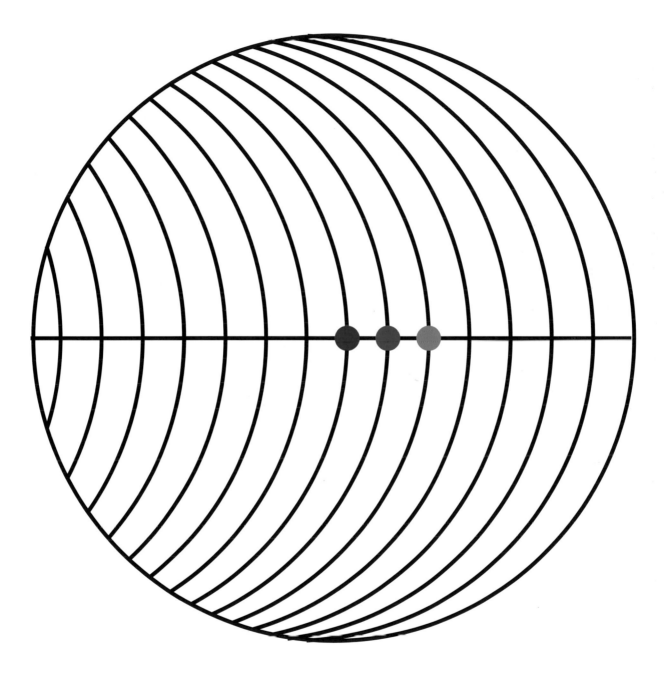

It doesn't look it, but the red dot is in the exact center. The curves trick us into thinking that the center is to the right of where it actually is!

SPOTS OF A DIFFERENT COLOR

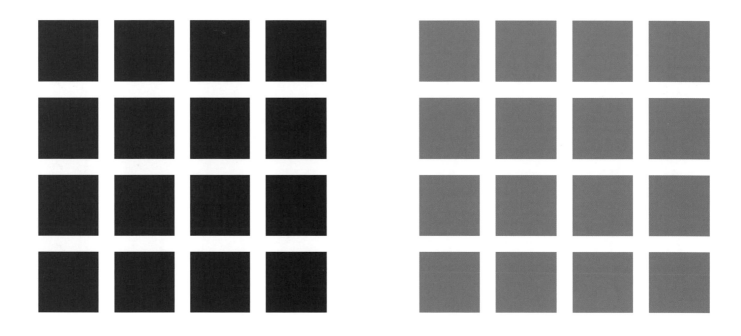

Look at the red and green blocks below.
What color spots dance at the corners of the pattern?

PERPLEXING PARALLEL PATTERNS

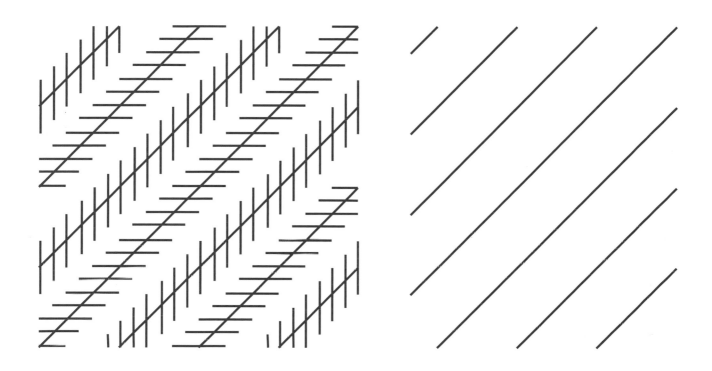

By themselves, the seven lines below seem perfectly parallel. No problem in seeing that. However, look what happens when you add a confusing pattern. The lines take on a new "leaning." Although the tilt may be new, the illusion isn't. It's based upon the Zollner illusion, which was first published in 1860.

COOL SHADES

place pencil here

Which side of the rectangle above is darker? Are you sure? Good. Now take a pencil and place it along the border, dividing the block in half. Now, which side is darker? Remove the pencil. What happens now?

See explanation on page 243

Optical Illusion Puzzles

In the upper left corner you will find a floor plan for a mountain. Which mountain landscape (A–C) does not correspond to the plan?

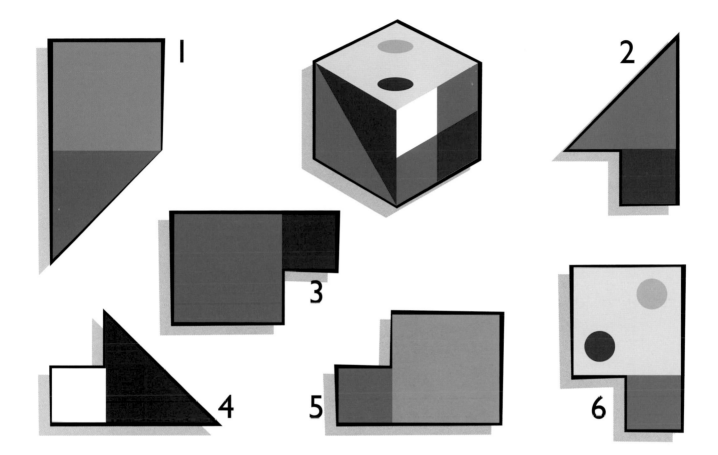

Which piece (1–6) is not needed to make the cube?

How many glasses of eggnog did the skier drink during his 2001 skiing holiday?

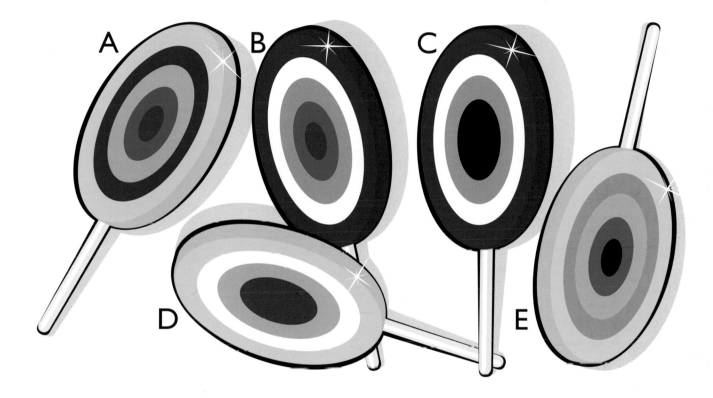

Three out of these five lollipops were made by the same candy factory. The factory has only seven different flavors for their lollipops. Which three lollipops are theirs?

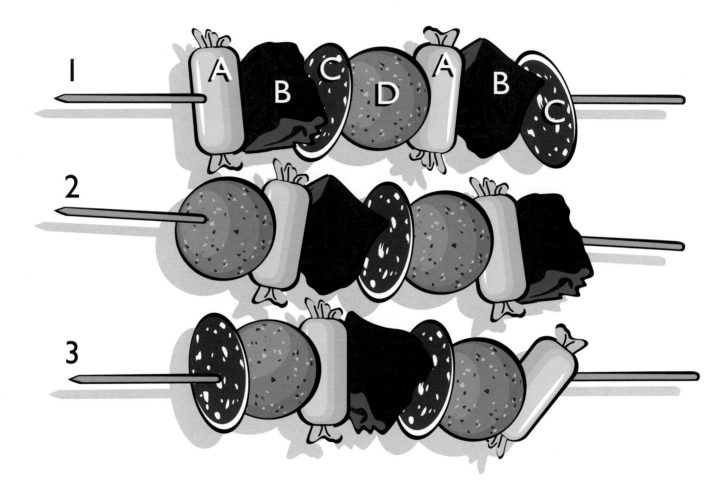

Four different kinds of meat were used to make these skewers consisting of seven pieces of meat. These are the first three skewers of a whole series. What will skewer 99 look like? Your answer will take the form of DABCDAB.

What number should replace the question mark?

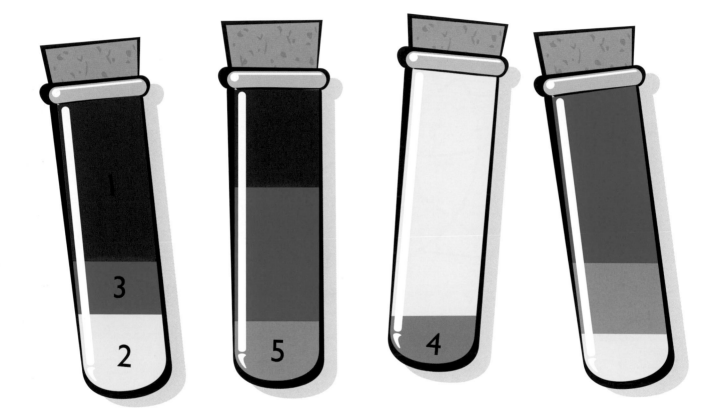

Which liquid (1–5) has the highest density?

What number is missing at the end of this series?

The wrong figures appear on the display of this broken calculator. When you enter the numbers 708510, the numbers 4105282740 actually appear on the display. How will the numbers 50364 be converted by the calculator?

What print (A–E) has not been made by the stamp?

Which cube is the same as the layout on the left?

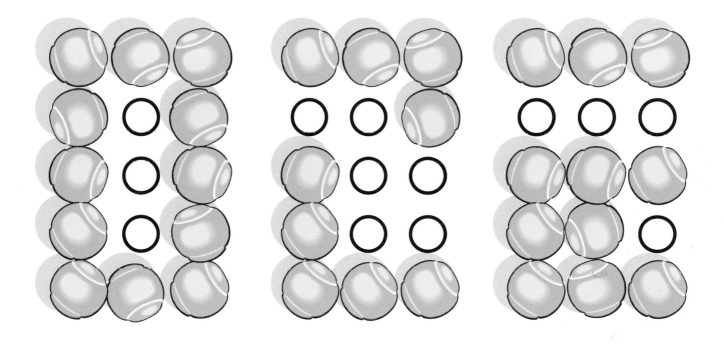

What tennis term do you get by moving one ball in each group?

Which one of the five pieces will complete the block?

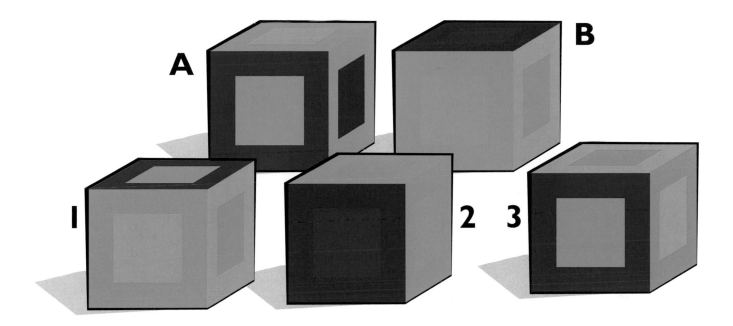

A and B are identical cubes that are seen from different sides. Therefore, you see all six sides of the cube. Which one of the three cubes (1, 2, or 3) is not a different view of the original cube?

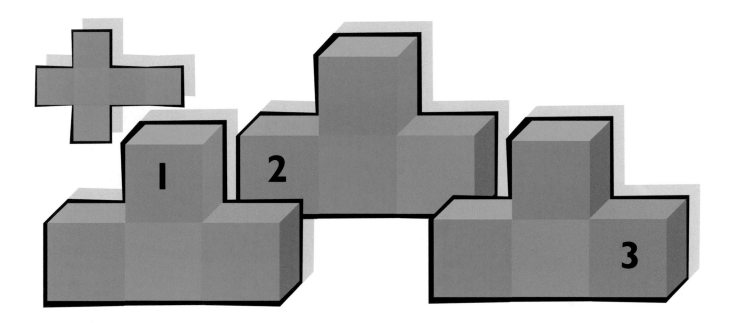

The illustration at the top left is the layout of an unfolded cube. Folding the cube and using it four times produces two out of these three daises. Which daises used a different cube?

The same ribbon is shown from different perspectives. Which ribbon (1–5) is wrong?

1

2

3

4

5

6

There are three pairs of skis here. Which numbers make up each pair?

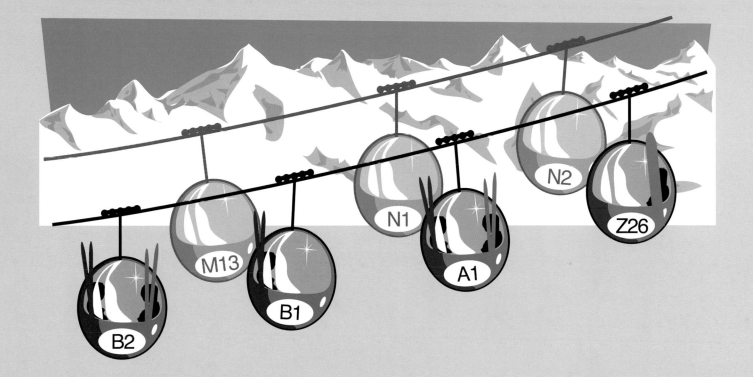

How many eggs are being moved by this ski lift?

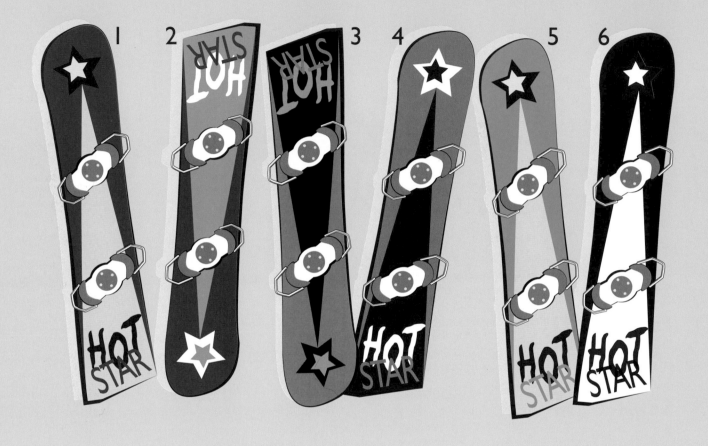

Which snowboard has a printing design error?

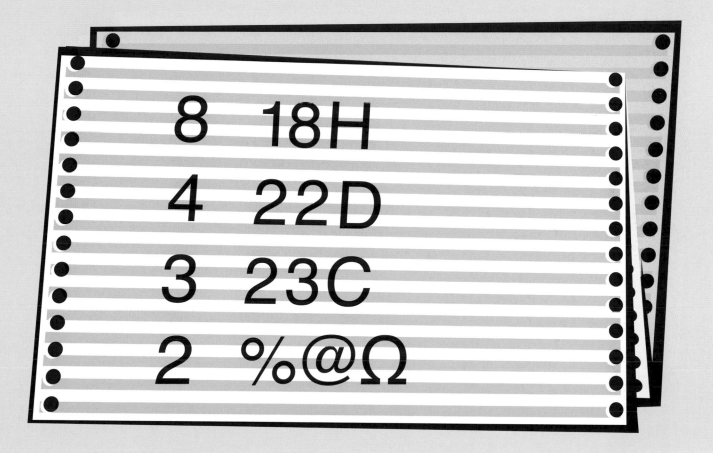

When asked to produce a listing of the pin codes for the numbers 8, 4, 3, and 2, the computer made a mistake in the case of a pin code for the number 2. What should be the correct pin code for 2?

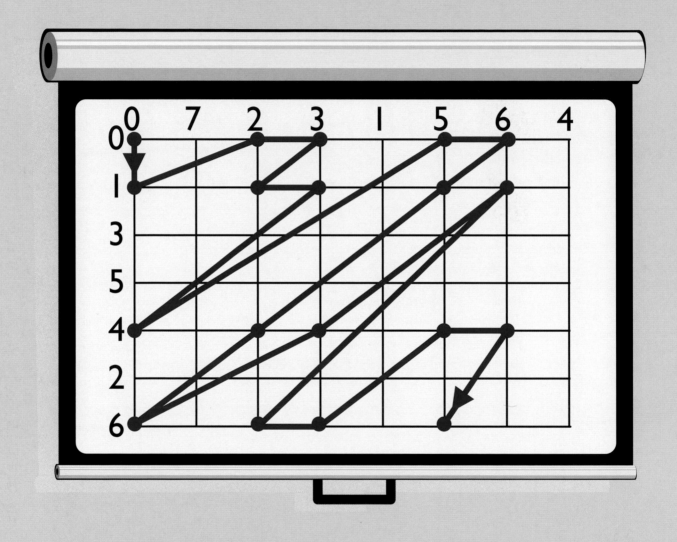

The graph is complete except for the endpoint. Indicate the coordinates of the endpoint by giving first a value of the horizontal axis and then a vertical value.

170

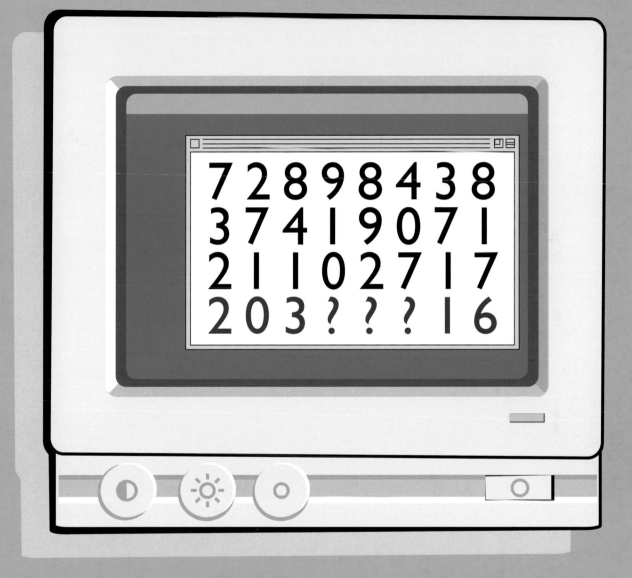

What three numbers are missing?

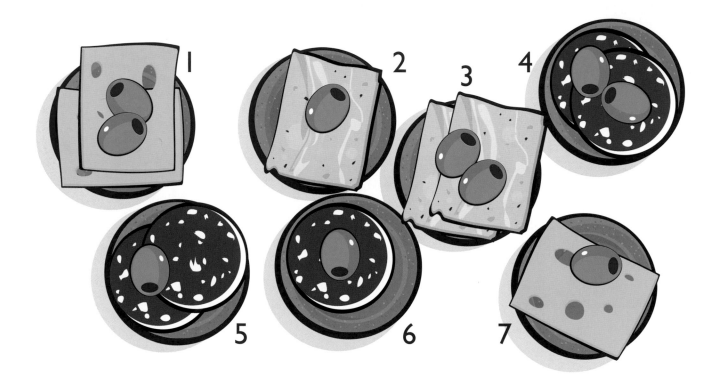

Which serving of bread is the odd one out?

How many buttons should there be on the body of the last snowman?

How many berries should there be on the last holly?

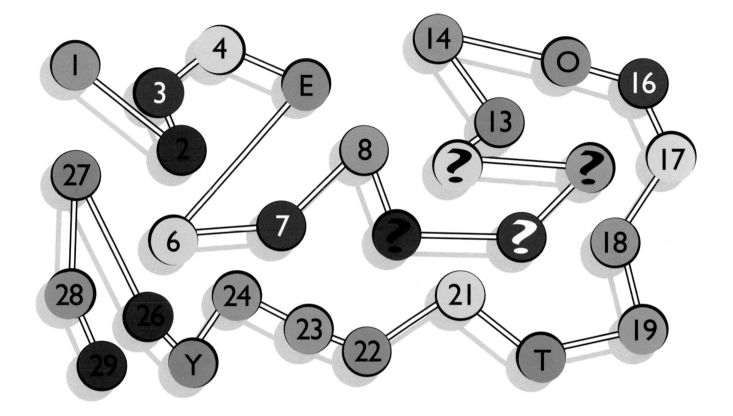

The carnival parade passes through four different points of a city. Which numbers (or letters) should replace the question marks?

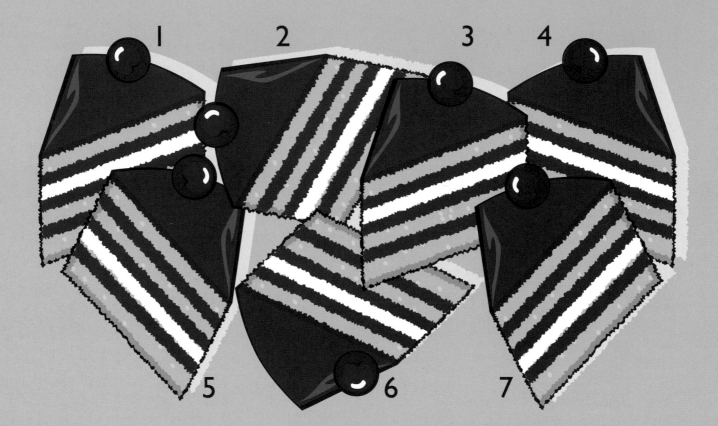

These are slices from three different cakes. There is only one slice from the third cake. Which slice is it?

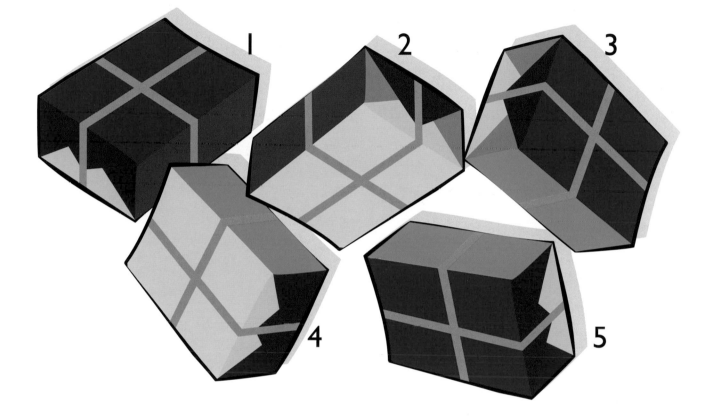

Which wrapping is the odd one out?

What coat of arms belongs to a different family?

Which stack of index cards is the odd one out?

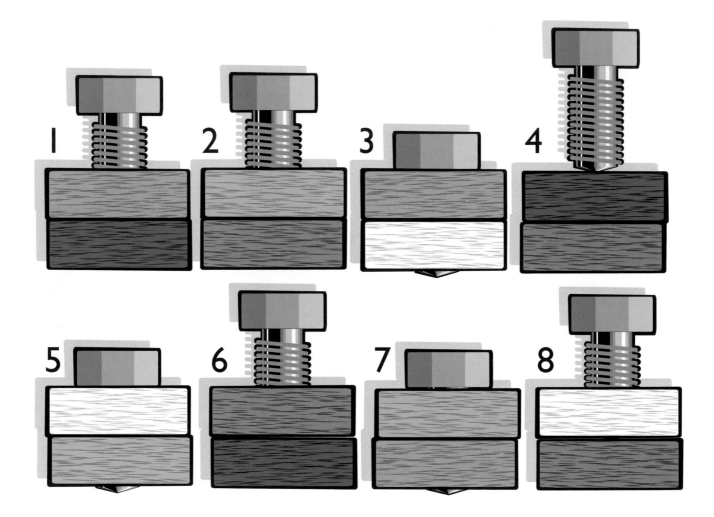

Certain blocks have threaded holes; others do not. All the blocks of the same color are identical and all the threaded bolts are equally long. Which set of blocks is incorrect?

Which arrow should be on the fifth key of the second row: L (left), R (right), LU (left upper), LB (left bottom), RU (right upper), or RB (right bottom)?

Which mask does not belong here?

Which flag (1–11) does not belong here?

What number should be on the next pair of shorts?

What number should replace the question mark?

Three out of the four caps have been made by the same company. The company used four different fabrics. Which cap didn't it make?

52?34

What number should replace the question mark?

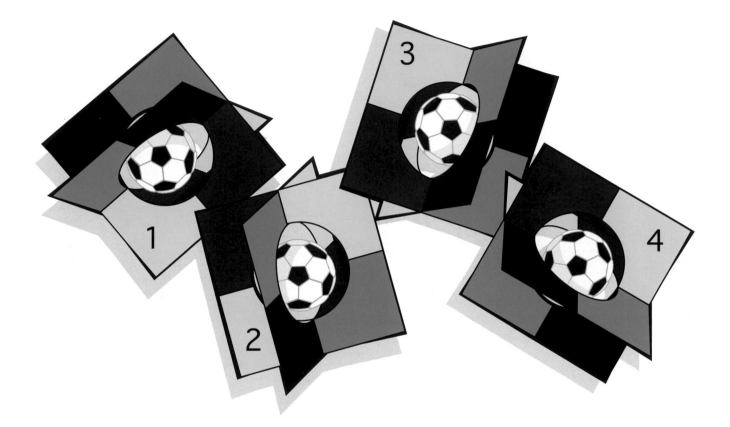

Which object is not identical to the others?

Which design does not belong in this set?

1822   2142   1914

The price for each set of medals is shown. How much does a bronze medal, which is part of the third set, cost?

The stonemason made a mistake on the design of this frieze. Indicate the row and the position of the mistake. For example, if there is a mistake on the sixth element of series B, the answer would be B6.

How many white dots should there be on the wings of the last ladybug?

If you turn Wheel A clockwise, which way will Wheel B turn—to the left (counterclockwise) or to the right (clockwise)?

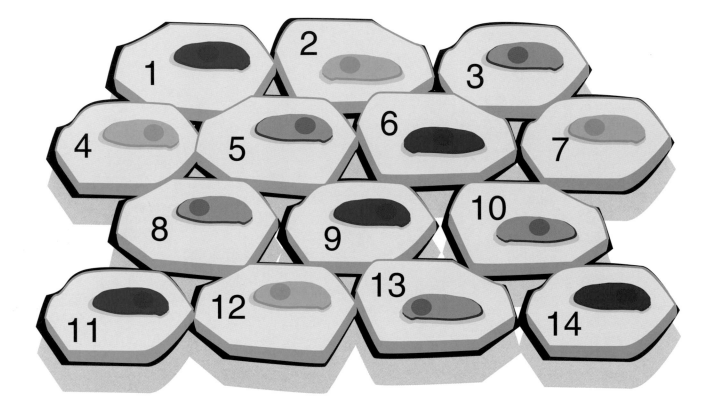

Which is the odd one out?

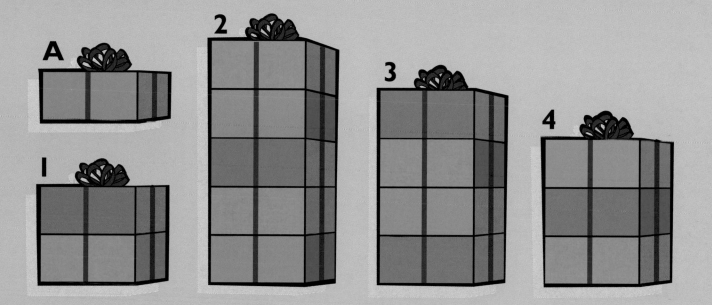

On what pile (1, 2, 3, or 4) is Brian going to put his last present (A)?

On each side of each cube is printed a different symbol. Each cube has the same six symbols. Which cube (1, 2, 3, or 4) is exactly the same as cube 0?

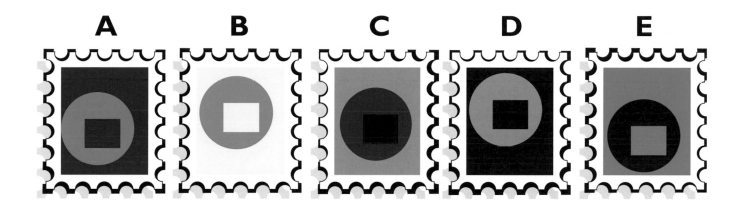

One of the stamps in this series does not fit in with the others. Which one is it?

The price of this ring keeps dropping. What price should be its price on the third tag?

Which of the three large patterns can be made with the small tile?

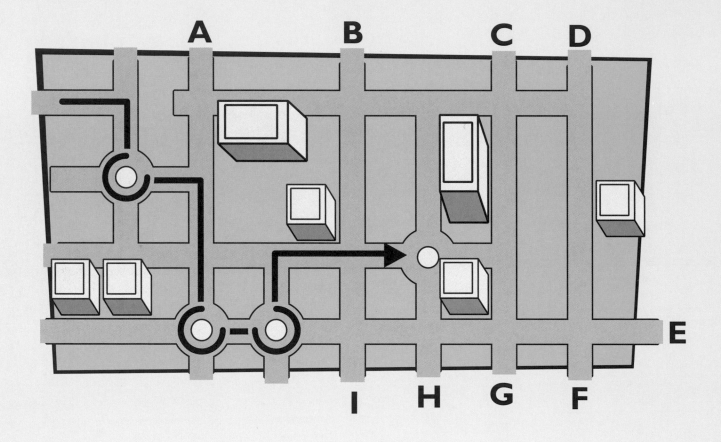

At which exit point will the marathon runner leave the city?

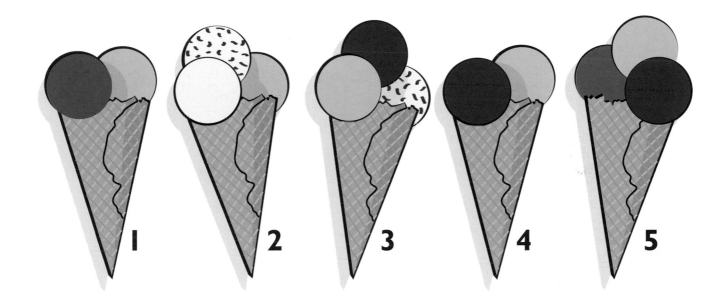

Brian bought four of the five ice creams from his usual ice cream store. The store has only four different flavors. Which ice cream (1, 2, 3, 4, or 5) did he buy someplace else?

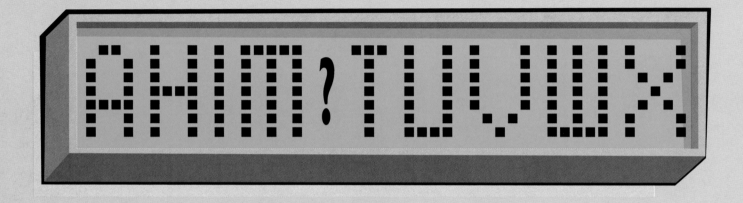

These nine letters of the alphabet belong together for a reason. Once you figure out the reason, find the missing letter.

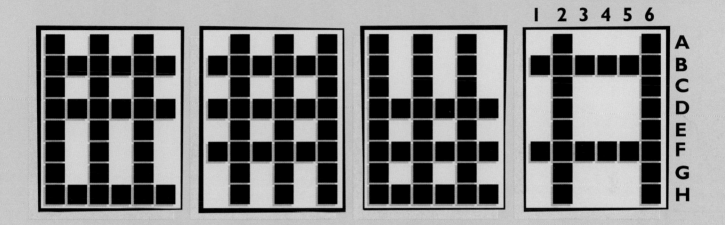

On this digital display, horizontal and vertical bars are shown. The bars follow a certain pattern. The last screen, however, broke down. Which vertical (1–6) and horizontal (A–H) bar should be there?

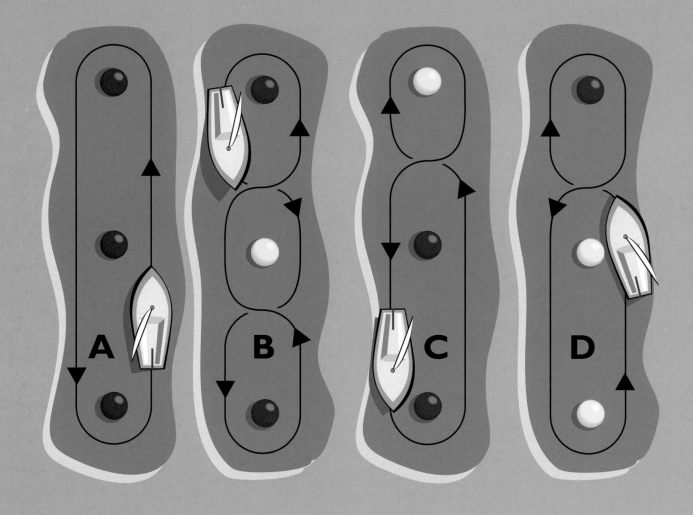

On which sailboat (A, B, C, or D) did the captain make a track error?

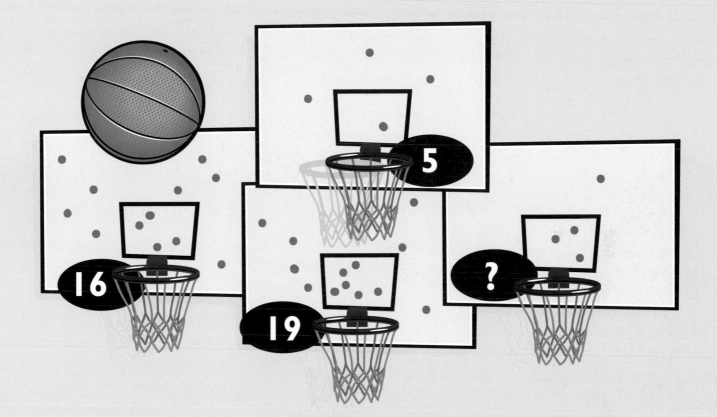

How many points were made at the fourth basket?

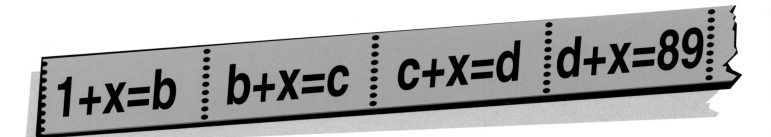

1+x=b | b+x=c | c+x=d | d+x=89

What is the value of x?

Four of the five ladybugs belong to the same species. Which ladybug is the odd one out? There can only be at most four different colors in one species of ladybug.

The cakes change each month. Cake 1 has been made in August, Cake 2 in June, and Cake 3 in May. In what month has Cake 4 been made?

The numbers on the keypad follow a certain logic. What number should replace the question mark?

The blackboard shows a series of numbers. What should the three missing numbers be?

Move just one single chalk line to complete the formula.

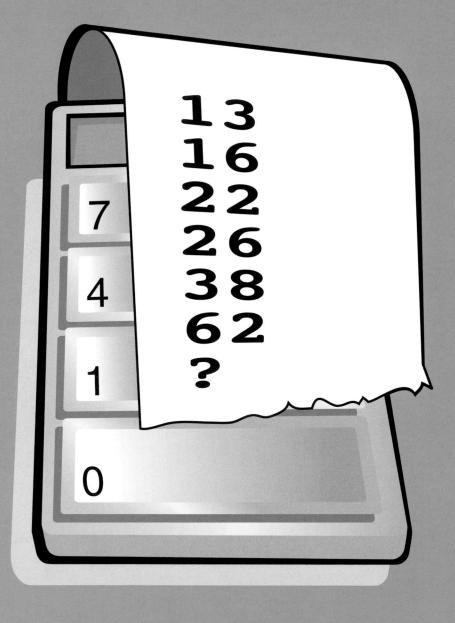

What number should replace the question mark?

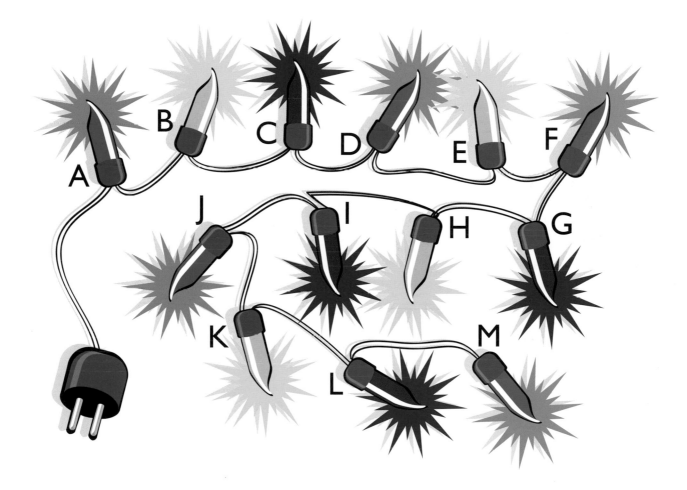

Which two lightbulbs need to be switched for the lights to follow a sequence?

How many red Christmas lights should be on the last tree?

These are all different views of the same die. The last die has a blank side. How many dots should be there?

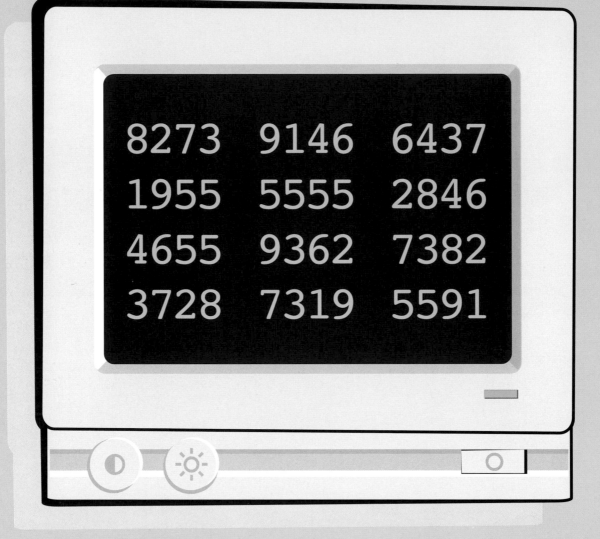

Which number does not belong here?

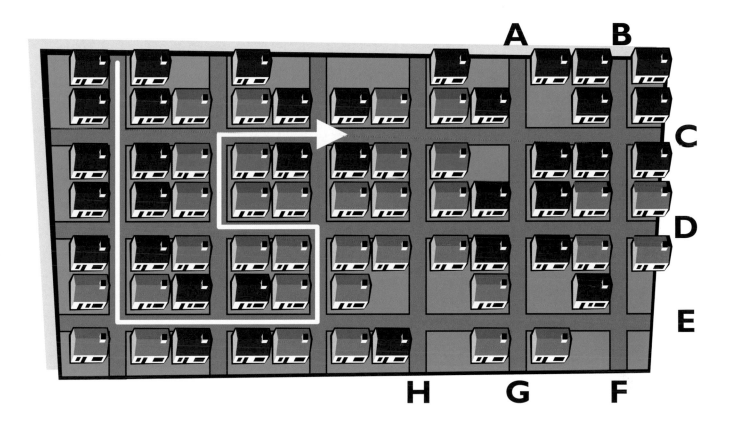

At which exit point will the messenger leave the city?

Which piece (1, 2, 3, 4, 5, 6, 7, or 8) should replace the question mark?

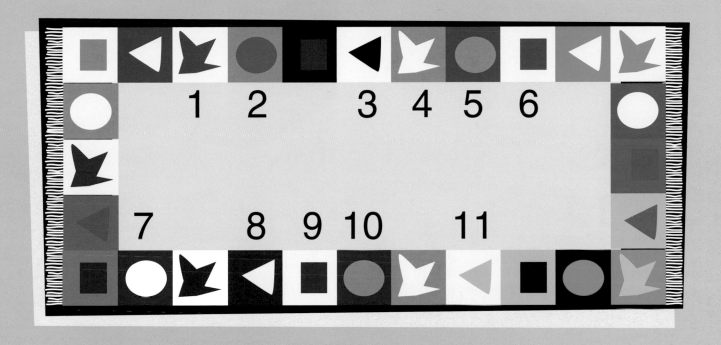

A mistake has been made in the pattern on this carpet. At which section (1–11) did the weaver make his mistake?

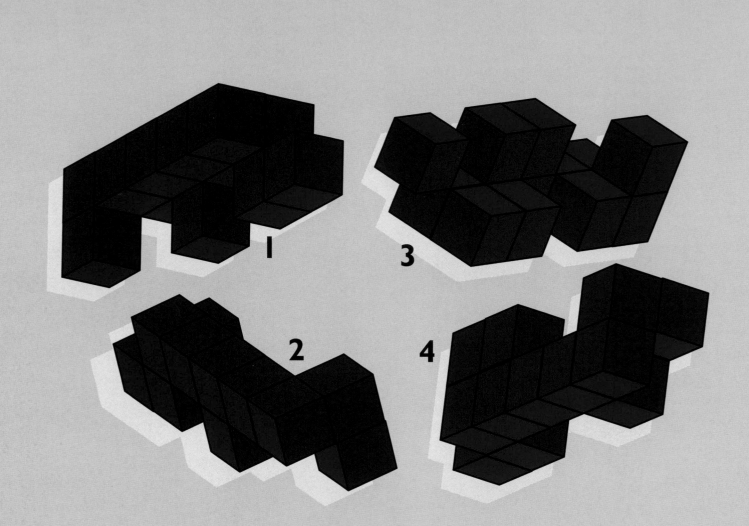

Which two elements constitute a perfect beam?

In what order should the last set of blocks be stacked? Indicate the numbers of the blocks in your answer (e.g., 122312), starting with the bottom block.

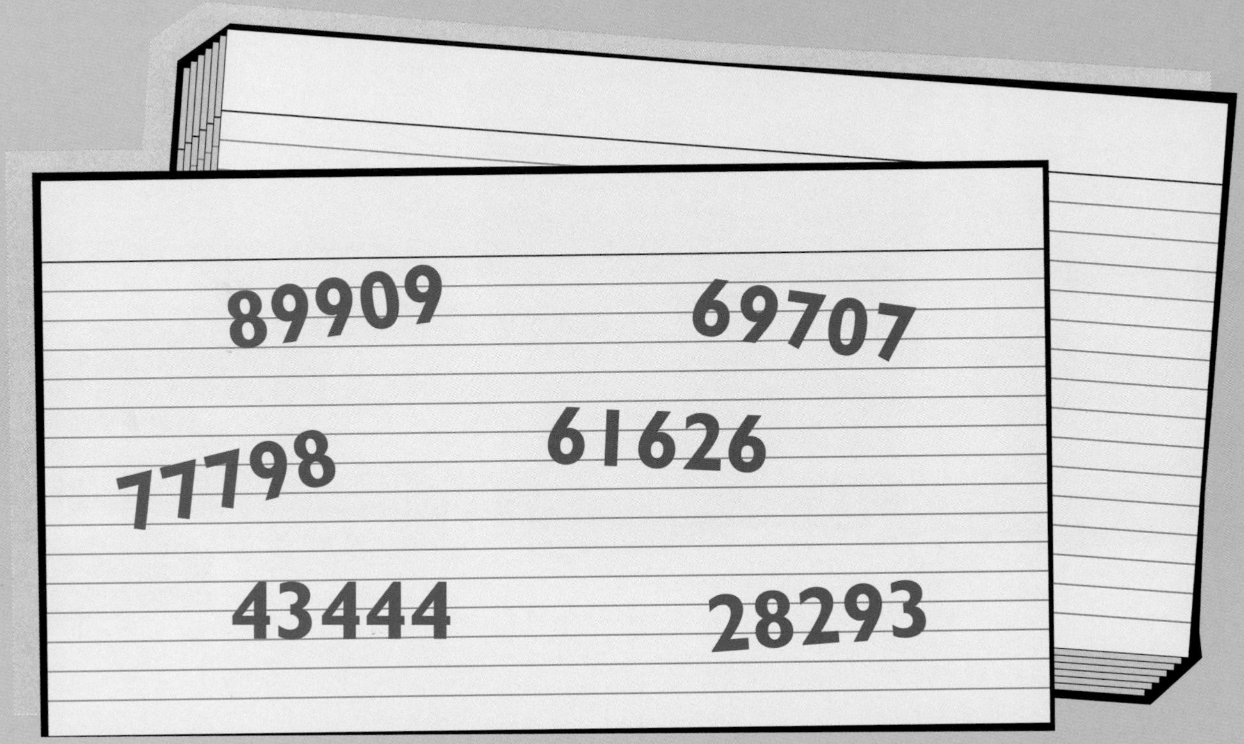

89909   69707

77798   61626

43444   28293

Which number does not fit with the others?

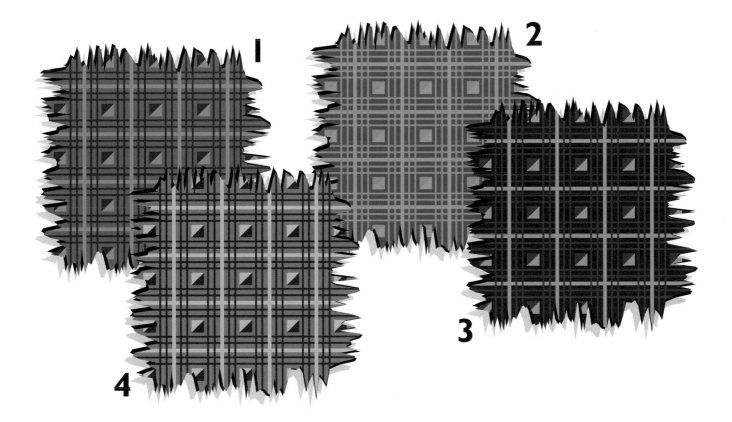

Which piece of fabric does not belong in the same Scottish family?

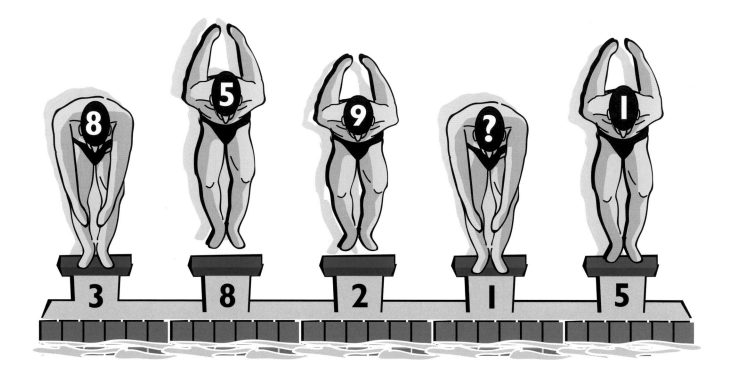

What number should be on the cap of the swimmer in lane 1?

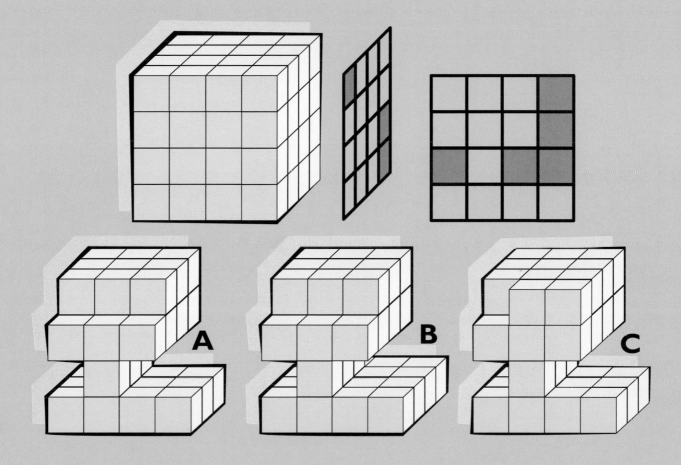

A piece of cheese successively passes through two molds. The cheese can only pass through the white squares. It moves from left to right through the first mold, and then from the back to the front through the second mold. Which piece of cheese will we be left with: A, B, or C?

$$\frac{3}{4} \quad \frac{4}{3} \quad \frac{6}{8} \quad \frac{24}{18} \quad \frac{72}{96} \quad \frac{?}{?}$$

What fraction will complete the series?

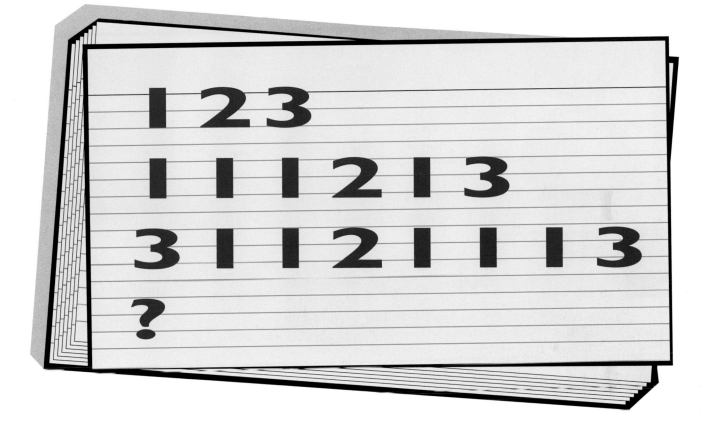

What will be the sequence of numbers on the last line?

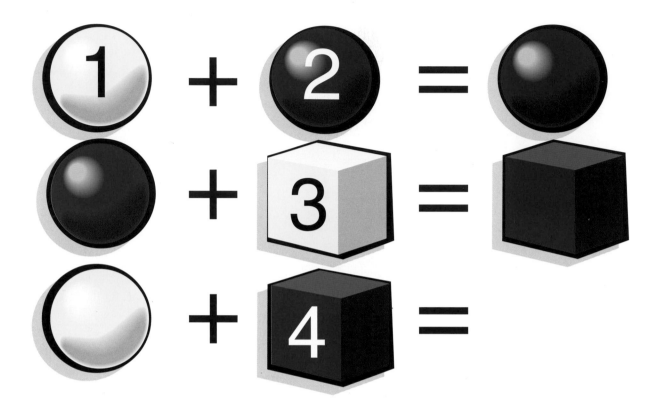

Just as in genetics, we find ourselves in the presence of dominants. Which element (1, 2, 3, or 4) is the result of the third operation?

This calculator is broken. The numbers on the keypad do not correspond with what appears on the display. If you press the numbers 4572301, the screen shows 1542630. If we press the number 89 on the keypad, what number will show up on the screen?

Solutions

Great Color Optical Illusions

Page 10

At first glance, you see a bearded man. On closer inspection, you'll find a phoenix.

Page 11

The zebra is descended from a solid black animal. The white stripes are superficial tufts on the black background color of the animal's skin.

Page 12

The drum appears to spin. The word "rotator" is a palindrome; it reads the same backwards and forwards.

Page 13

The old lady's face shows her life. You can see her as a baby, a young girl, courting, in marriage, and finally in death. This type of art is based on the work of Archimboldo, a painter who lived in Italy from 1517 to 1593.

Page 14

Turn the page upside down to see them smiling. Now they are married.

Page 15

The young woman's chin becomes the nose of the old lady.

Page 16

Bring the page close to your face. The bee and flower will come together.

Page 17

The circle appears to be in two different shades of color.

Page 18

The Three of Hearts (tree of hearts).

Page 19
Mona Lisa.

Page 20
The secret word is "hello." Look at the page in the direction of the arrow at eye level.

Page 21
Look closely and you'll find the profiles of Adam and Eve. The phrase "Madam I'm Adam" is a palindrome; it reads the same backwards and forwards.

Page 22
It looks like an old Asian man. Daniel Webster's shirt forms his forehead.

Page 23
The letter E. Try looking at the page from a distance.

Page 24
It changes direction!

Page 25
Turn the page upside down and you will see a slice of cake. The name "Otto" has both horizontal and vertical symmetry. And it's also a palindrome!

Page 26
They are both the same size. Trace one of them and measure it against the other. Their curve tricks us and creates the illusion.

Page 27
It is a magic square. Each horizontal, vertical, and diagonal line of four numbers adds up to 264. It also works if you turn it upside down.

Page 28
It's a crate. Look at the illustration. It's easier to see it with the added lines.

Page 29
It all depends on how you look at it.

Page 30
A black cat down a coal mine eating a stick of licorice at midnight.

Page 31
Pile B. Were you surprised? Measure each of them to check.

Page 32
It appears to follow you, but it's just an illusion. This design was used as a recruiting poster for the British Army.

Page 33
Turn the page upside down.

Page 34
Each circle will seem to revolve on its axis. The inner cog wheel will appear to rotate in the opposite direction.

Page 35
The message, made up from the pale background shapes, says, "Can you find the words."

Page 36
Turn the page upside down and you will see the mother's head. The baby's diaper becomes the mother's head scarf.

Page 37
The face can belong to either the man or the woman.

Page 38
Turn the page upside down.

Page 39
The right eye and bridge of the nose form the heads of Romeo and Juliet. This form of art was popular in the 19th century in Europe.

Page 40
Look at the reflection of this page in the mirror.

Page 41
It says, "We see but we we don't observe."

Page 42
A part of Hearn's act is shown close-up. From a distance, it resembles the performer.

Page 43
A person riding a horse. See the illustration.

Page 44
Take your pick!

Page 45
The choice is yours!

Page 46
The choice is yours. It all depends on what you saw first. Horizontally, it reads A, B, C. Vertically, it reads 12, 13, 14.

Page 47
Turn the page upside down. Then look at the reflection in a mirror and you will see the correct price is only 20¢.

Page 48
Bring the page closer to your face. The figures will come together.

Page 49
It says, "I've got a a big head."

Page 50
Look at the left side of the picture and you will see the profile of the farmer's face.

Page 51
Look at the markings on the cow's back. You will see a map of the United Kingdom.

Page 52
There are six F's in the sentence.

Page 53
Turn the page 90° counterclockwise.

Page 54
See the illustration.

Page 55
"X" marks their spot. See illustration.

Page 56
Turn the page 90° counterclockwise. His face will appear.

Page 57
Napoleon's silhouette is found between the two trees on the right.

Page 58
Look at the lion's mane. You will see some of the old British colonies: Canada, India, Australia, New Zealand, and African colonies.

Page 59
It is supposed to be the longest sentence that still reads the same when you turn it upside down.

Page 60
Your guess is as good as mine. It's impossible to tell.

Page 61
Look at the sequence of the words. It says, "the with." It should be "with the."

Page 62
The three donkeys have only three ears among them!

Page 63
The choice is yours. Did you notice that the caption says, "How many can can you see?"

Page 64
Turn on the light. It's an impossible candelabra. A number of the holders seem to be suspended in midair.

Page 65
The middle leg is impossible.

Page 66
The previous one was 1881. The next one will occur in the year 6009.

Page 67
Turn the page upside down and it says, "Lots o' eggs."

Page 68
The shapes spell the word "eye." The shelf is an impossible object.

Page 69
To tie mules to.

Page 70
You will see a lightbulb with a glowing yellow center. Yellow is the reverse color to blue. These opposite colors are known as complementary colors.

Page 71
It says, "Optical illusions are magic."

Page 72
It depends on what direction you see the bird flying. Either answer is correct.

Page 73
Turn the page 90° clockwise to reveal the circus.

Page 74
It's a dog curled up on a rug. Turn the page so that the arrow points upwards to reveal the dog.

Page 75
Study the picture carefully and you'll see his face. His hat is formed from the dog's ear.

Page 76
Yes, it's impossible. Count the number of steps. You can count three, nine, or five steps.

Page 77
The blue dot that is on the line is in the center.

Page 78
The star is midway between the point and the base. Use a ruler and you'll see.

Page 79
You might see a medal or two people having an argument.

Page 80
No. The set of stairs is impossible.

Page 81
They are both the same height. The lines of perspective help to create the illusion of one being taller than the other.

Page 82
At first glance, we think he's happy. But he's really sad. We are not used to seeing faces upside down. Since the mouth and eyes have been inverted, he seems very weird when we look at him.

Page 83
The fourth one down reads "something."

Page 84
Turn the page upside down and he looks exactly the same.

Page 85
Turn the page 90° counterclockwise.

Page 86
From a distance, it's a skull. Close up, it's a man and woman sitting at a table.

Page 87
Turn the page upside down for the answer. It says "Life."

Hints and Explanations

Optical Illusion Magic

Tricky Tracks (page 118)
You may need a ruler to check this out, but the two dinosaurs are the exact same size! Your brain followed the short cut and got lost.

Comparison Concepts (pages 120 & 121)
The center squares on page 120 are the same size just as the center circles on page 121 are equal in size. Your brain is constantly comparing things. It was tricked into thinking that the center square (bottom of page 120) and the center circle (top of page 121) were each bigger because they were larger than the surrounding objects. At the same time, it was tricked into thinking that the center square (top of page 120) and the center circle (bottom of page 121) were smaller, since they appeared smaller than the surrounding objects. Your brain used this concept to create an unfair comparison.

After Images (pages 126, 127, 142, 143)
After images are illusions that appear after your vision has been overstimulated. Over-simulation can be caused by a camera's bright flash—those floating spots are after images! After images can also be caused by staring at the same thing for a long period of time.

As you look at an object, the light that falls on your retina alters the chemistry balance of your eye. This change temporarily "imprints" a kind of image on your retina. When you look away from the object, you see its afterimage illusion. Although it's the same size and shape, it "materializes" in opposite shades (like a black-and-white photographic negative).

Hint: New Outlook (page 136)
To uncover the overhang, turn the image on page 136 upside down. Once this new staircase "materializes," slowly rotate the page back to its upright position. This technique can help produce the overhang. Don't give up. It will take some practice to keep the overhang from "flipping" back to steps.

Cool Shades (page 148)
What Happened? It's the special shading of the adjacent blocks that creates this powerful illusion. Both halves are identical. However, they are not filled with a single shade of gray. Each half contains a gradual change from light gray to dark gray. This type of change is called a gradient. The dividing line forms where the dark border of the left half meets the light border of the right half. When this margin is uncovered, you can easily detect the difference in shades. However, when it gets covered by the pencil, your brain gets confused. It can't detect a distinct edge and mistakenly assumes that each block is filled with its own uniform shade of gray.

Solutions

Optical Illusion Puzzles

Page 150
Landscape A does not belong.

Page 151
Piece number 2.

Page 152
Three. The sum of the figures of the year equals the number of glasses of eggnog the skier had.

Page 153
A, B, and D. If you add C and/or E to the other lollipops, you end up with eight different flavors.

Page 154
After four skewers, the order of the pieces of meat is repeated: ABCDABC, DABCDAB, CDABCDA, BCDABCD. The 100th skewer will follow the fourth order of meat (4 x 25=100). That is why the 99th skewer will be the third-order combination—i.e., CDABCDA.

Page 155
5. Starting at 2 and going clockwise, the sequence of numbers is carried out by +1, +2, +3, +4, +5.

Page 156
Liquid 4. The liquid with the highest density is to be found at the bottom of the test tube. Here you have the liquids in order of density: 1, 3, 5, 2, 4.

Page 157
20. Starting with the first number (4), the sequence of numbers is carried out by x1, −2, x3, −4, x5, −6, x7, −8.

Page 158
820969371. It is clear that only the number 0 is correctly reproduced. When you enter one of the other numbers, the two accompanying numbers in the

you enter one of the other numbers, the two accompanying numbers in the same column appear on the display. For instance, if you enter the number 5, then 82 will be shown on the display.

Page 159
Print E. The middle line has shifted.

Page 160
Cube number 3.

Page 161
ACE.

Page 162
All five pieces fit perfectly into the block. But piece number 2 is the only one that has the correct colors.

Page 163
Cube 2. The blue frame on the top side should be orange in order for the cube to be identical with the original cube.

Page 164
Dais 2. The cube at the far right does not match the layout.

Page 165
Ribbon number 3 is wrong.

Page 166
1-3, 2-6, 4-5. The design patterns are the same on the right and left skis of each pair.

Page 167
351. The numerical position of a letter in the alphabet tells you the number of egg lifts corresponding to that letter. For example, A corresponds to one lift, B to two lifts, and so on until 26 egg lifts for the letter Z. In total, the lift will have 351 eggs.

Page 168
Snowboard 3. On all the other snowboards, the word "HOT" is the same color as the big star and the triangle is the same color as the small star.

Page 169
24B. The pin code is found using this formula: The digit is 26 minus the number. The letter is the place of the number in the alphabet. For example: The pin code for 8 is 26 − 8 = 18, and the eighth letter of the alphabet, H: 18H.

Page 170
(6,6). The line of the graph connects only those points of which the values are labeled correctly. On the horizontal axis those values are 0, 2, 3, 5, and 6. On the vertical axis they are 0, 1, 4, and 6. The only point that remains to connect is (6,6).

Page 171
091. Each number is the second digit of the sum of the other numbers in the same column. In the first column, 9 + 1 + 0 = 10, and we keep the 0. The second column: 8 + 9 + 2 = 19, and we keep the 9. And finally, 4 + 0 + 7 = 11, and we keep the 1.

Page 172
5. All the other servings have as many olives as they have slices of cold cuts.

Page 173
7. Every snowman has the same number of buttons on its face as on its body.

Page 174
3. The number of the berries and leaves always totals 8.

Page 175
9, J, 11, and 12. The points go in numerical order from 1 to 29. Each fifth point is replaced by the letter of the alphabet that occupies that numerical position.

Page 176
Slice number 6 is from the third cake because the cherry is in the middle of the cake.

Page 177
Wrapping number 5. In order for it to be identical with the other wrappings, the green side should be purple.

Page 178
4. All the other coats of arms use the same three colors. Coat 4 only uses two colors.

Page 179
Stack C. In all the other stacks, the order of the colors is yellow, light green, gray, white, and pink.

Page 180
6. Sets 2 and 8 tell you that the red block has not been threaded.

Page 181
RU (right upper). All the arrows are part of smaller or larger endless loops.

Page 182
Mask number 4. In all the other masks, the right eye has moved 180° in relation to the left eye.

Page 183
Flag number 8. The left part of each flag has the color sequence black, blue, yellow, and red. The right part has the color sequence red, white, and black. So the right half of flag number 8 should be white.

Page 184
22. The number of the next shorts is the number of the previous shorts plus the number in the black rectangle.

Page 185
20. The sum of the numbers of the same-colored chairs is always 25.

Page 186
Cap number 3. To have made cap number 3 would have taken five different fabrics.

Page 187
7. Each number represents the number of identically colored soccer balls.

Page 188
Object number 2.

Page 189
Design 4. All the other designs have a red ring at the bottom.

Page 190
92. A silver medal costs 320 (2142 − 1822). A gold medal costs 1502 (1822 − 320). Consequently, the bronze medal costs 1914 − 320 − 1502 = 92.

Page 191
B3.

Page 192
Three. The difference between the number of black and white dots is always two. The last ladybug should have three white dots.

Page 193
Wheel B will turn to the left (counterclockwise).

Page 194
10. The row of cells follows the color sequence red, orange, and lavender. Cell number 10 does not follow that sequence.

Page 195
Pile 3. Brian's piles follow a color scheme: Orange, green, and blue always succeed each other in the same order. In doing so, he has considered both the front and side of the piles. The only pile he can put his last present on is pile 3.

Page 196
Cube 2.

Page 197
Stamp C is the only stamp in which the little square does not have the same color as its background.

Page 198
$8100. Each time the price drops by 10%.

Page 199
All three patterns can be made with this tile. Imagine a ticktacktoe box over each pattern and you will see how the tile fits.

Page 200
F. At each T-intersection, the marathon runner makes a right. At each circular point, he goes to the left, and, at each crossroad, he runs straight. Following this pattern, the runner will be leaving the city at point F.

Page 201
2. The only flavor his usual store does not have is vanilla.

Page 202
O. In our alphabet, ten letters are their own mirror image. Therefore, the missing letter is O.

Page 203
Row H and column 4. The vertical bars move one step to the right per screen, and the horizontal bars two steps down. The last screen should show the vertical bar in position 4 and the horizontal line in position H.

Page 204
Track D. The red buoy must be taken on the left-hand side and the yellow buoy on the right-hand side.

Page 205
7. The score is equal to the total number of marks plus the marks put inside the small square.

Page 206
22. $b = x + 1$, $b + x = c$; so $x + 1 + x = c$ or $c = 2x + 1$. $c + x = d$; so $2x + 1 + x = d$ or $d = 3x + 1$. $d + x = 89$; so $3x + 1 + x = 89$. To solve for x: $4x + 1 = 89$, $4x = 88$, $x = 22$.

Page 207
Ladybug number 2.

Page 208
April. The number of chocolate lines on the cakes indicates the month.

Page 209
8. The sum of each row and each column equals 15.

Page 210
6, 9, and 8. The numbers are alternately added and subtracted: $2 + 3 = 5$; $5 - 1 = 4$; $4 + 6 = 10$, etc.

Page 211
Move the fourth chalk line in order to end up with the square root of one. $\sqrt{1} = 1$.

Page 212
74. Each number is the sum of the number in the previous row plus the product of its digits: $13 + (1 \times 3)$, $16 + (1 \times 6)$, $22 + (2 \times 2)$, $26 + (2 \times 6)$, $38 + (3 \times 8)$, $62 + (6 \times 2) = 74$.

Page 213
Switch lightbulbs F and G and the color sequence is blue, yellow, and red.

Page 214
3. The sum of the yellow and blue lights equals the number of red lights.

Page 215
6 dots.

Page 216
9362. With all the other numbers, the first two and the last two digits always add up to ten.

Page 217
B. At each intersection where there are four red rooftops, the messenger goes straight. At each intersection where there are four gray rooftops, he turns left; at four green rooftops, he turns right. Following this pattern, he will leave the city at point B.

Page 218
6. Follow a spiral that unfolds towards the center.

Page 219
2. The figure inside each square has the color of the preceding square.

Page 220
Elements 1 and 2.

Page 221
From bottom to top: 311222. The most same-colored blocks are stacked on top.

Page 222
77798. All the numbers can be read as follows: 89 90 9(1), 69 70 7(1), 28 29 3(0), etc.

Page 223

4. The color of the thick lines is different from the color of the bottom triangle.

Page 224

7. The number on the cap is the sum of the numbers of the neighboring lanes: 2 + 5 = 7.

Page 225
Piece A.

Page 226

480/360. The numerator and denominator of each fraction are multiplied by their position in the series. The product of the numerator becomes the denominator in the next fraction and the product of the denominator becomes the numerator in the next fraction. To get the last fraction of the series, the numerator (72) of the fifth fraction is multiplied by its position (5) to give you the denominator of the next fraction. The denominator (96) is multiplied by its position (5) to give you the numerator of the next fraction.

Page 227

1321123113. Each line is a literal translation of the contents of the previous line. For example: To get the numbers of the second line, the previous line has one 1, one 2, and one 3—or, 111213. The next line has three 1s, one 2, one 1, and one 3—or, 31121113. For the last line, we have one 3, two 1s, one 2, three 1s, and one 3: 1321123113.

Page 228

4. From the first operation, it appears red is the dominant color. From the second operation, it appears that, apart from the color red, the cube is the dominant shape. Consequently, the third operation will produce a red cube.

Page 229

78. The numbers around 5 and 2 move forward one position clockwise. Therefore, 89 will show up as 78 on the screen.